HOW TO HAVE
A MEANINGFUL
RELATIONSHIP
WITH YOUR
COMPUTER

Sandy Berger

Sunstar
PUBLISHING LTD.

HOW TO HAVE A MEANINGFUL RELATIONSHIP
WITH YOUR COMPUTER
by Sandy Berger

© United States Copyright, 1997
Computer Living Corp.
PO Box 2007
Pinehurst, NC 28370
HTTP://www.compukiss.com

Cover Design: John Buck
Illustrations: John Buck

LCCN: 97-065715
ISBN: 1-887472-36-3
First Printing, 1997
Printed in the U.S.A.

Sunstar Publishing, Ltd.
116 North Court
Fairfield, Iowa 52556

To my husband,

who taught me to believe in myself and

encouraged me to share my knowledge

with the world.

Acknowledgements

The process of living is like trying to use a new computer program without any manual or instructions. You use a method based on trial and error and learn from others as much as you can. I have been blessed to have many people in my life that I have not only learned from, but who have also supported and encouraged me.

Without my husband Dave, this book would never have been written. He is my most vocal supporter and has constantly guided and encouraged me in a positive and loving way throughout our relationship. I could never thank him enough for always being there for me.

Thanks to my parents, Roy and Edna Truschke, who gave me a proper start in this world by supplying a massive amount of love and guidance. They made me realize and understand that the important things in life are often unseen.

My children, Marybeth, Brenda and Michael are my greatest treasures in this world. They motivated me to write this book and supported me throughout the entire writing process.

John Buck is the creative talent behind the lively little cartoon character that we call PC Mac-Doodle. Many thanks go to John for his graphic contribution as well as for making himself constantly available for assistance.

Special thanks to MaryAnn Panek, Rodney Charles and Elizabeth Pacso for their editorial acumen and unfailing guidance.

Table of Contents

Foreward

Computers are for everyone. In my computer consulting business over the past thirty years, I have encountered many people who both wanted and needed to learn more about how to use a computer. My students have included computer neophytes as well as experienced computer users. Despite differences in their ages and educational backgrounds they all had one thing in common. They realized that it is becoming increasingly difficult to live in this technologically advanced world without having the necessary computer skills. Many people are thrown into the computer world without the proper foundation. They may use computers every day and still not be completely comfortable with them.

During my years of teaching I have been able to develop a way of explaining complex computer terminology in every day language. This book was written to give you a firm foundation in the world of computers, and to enhance both your productivity and your enjoyment of computers.

You will learn to get the most out of your computer experiences. The knowledge gained from this book will give you the confidence and the substance to expand your use of the computer and to remove the impediments to the world of technology. This book also includes several valuable resource sections including hardware and software manufacturer hot lines for help, recommended software products, a glossary of computer terms and a personal computer diary where you can document your computer-related purchases.

Owning this book is like having your own computer consultant at your fingertips.

Happy computing!

Introduction

Do you need a book that will quickly get you up and running in the computer world? Would you like an easy reference guide as you continue to grow into the new computer culture? What you usually find on bookshelves is: 1) high-tech references designed to explain the ins and outs of specific software programs, or 2) books titled *Dummy* or *Idiot* that prey on the normal insecurities people experience when they try something new.

Compu-KISS recognizes that you are neither a dummy nor an idiot. You are an intelligent person who is looking for a simple, positive way of interacting with your computer.

A computer, after all, is just a machine. Remember—human intelligence is what created the computer. Once you understand how that intelligence is applied to a computer, you can use the computer to enhance and empower your life.

"Make everything as simple as possible, but not simpler."

— *Albert Einstein*

Compu-KISS simplifies the world of computers and gives you the knowledge and confidence you need to get you where you want to be in the new technological age. It gives you the tools you need to understand the fundamentals of the computer world. This will allow you to be a part of the technical ideas and products of the future.

The name Compu-KISS is an acronym for:
The Computer World—Keeping It Short and Simple

Compu-KISS simplifies the world of computers by helping you remove the mystery. As the computer becomes less and less of a mysterious object, you will begin to form a positive and useful relationship with your computer.

Meaningful relationships generally evolve over time as the participants learn about and understand each other. Compu-KISS will help you learn enough about the computer to understand how it functions. Although the computer will never understand you on a personal level, it will respond to you and to the commands you give it. As you learn how to communicate with your computer, it will present you with the desired results. You will create a relationship with your computer that will make your life simpler and more rewarding.

 • **Compu-KISS has been designed to help you overcome your frustration with computers.**

 • **It will take the apprehension out of purchasing computer hardware and software.**

 • **It will give you the knowledge you need to get the computer to do what <u>you</u> want it to do.**

 • **It will help you fully utilize the power of computers to enhance your daily life.**

And now, come join us in the
Compu-KISS*
World of Computers

Discovering Your Personal Power With Computers

◆

Chapter 1

" Invading armies can be resisted...but nothing can resist an idea whose time has come."

— Victor Hugo

Computers have become an integral part of our daily lives. We are awakened in the morning by the radio station, which does all of its programming by computer. We check out the current story by our favorite columnist in the newspaper. Of course, this was written on a word processor and printed on computer-run presses. Then we drive to work in our car, which has its own computerized parts for various components throughout the vehicle. There are ATMs, VCRs and many computer-type machines in our daily lives. Certainly we are already immersed in the world of computers.

But what about the future? Our vision of the future is limited only by our imagination. It's certain that computers will play a primary role.

As with any major change in society, you can choose to be an observer and let the current take you wherever it may, or you can jump in a boat, grab a paddle and use the current to your advantage. If you choose to jump into the computer world now, you will reap many benefits and you will be able to take advantage of all that the computer world offers.

"To conquer fear is the beginning of wisdom."

— *Bertrand Russell*

Joining the Computer Revolution

The computer revolution began in earnest a short twenty years ago and is now taking on a culture of its own that is global in scope. The speed and dynamics of the changes caused by computers have left many people on the sidelines. They experience a resistance to computers brought on by an element of fear commonly referred to as technophobia, or the fear of technology. You may have just a little technophobia, or you may have a lot.

I have tutored people and actually heard their stomachs turn over in fear when they sit down in front of a computer. Many people who use a computer every day in their jobs are paralyzed by the idea of trying a new program. Wherever you fit in this scenario, don't worry. It's human nature to want to stay within your own comfort zone. With the knowledge and confidence that you gain from this book, you will be able to try new things and become an active part of our new computer culture.

Reading this book is the first step of your journey into the computer world.

Speaking of journeys, do you remember what it was like the first time you sat behind the wheel of a car to learn to drive? Chances are it was both exciting and scary. You couldn't wait to get onto the road, but you weren't exactly sure how to go about it.

Well, that's how we feel about computers: Today's computer culture is both exciting and scary. It's exciting when you think of all the wonderful things computers can do for your life, and it's scary because the rapidly changing technology always seems to be a little bit beyond your grasp.

Cars are often referred to as extensions of ourselves and our personalities. A person who drives a sports car might not want to be caught in a pickup truck and vice versa.

Just as cars can be extensions of ourselves, computers can be extensions of our minds. People use computers to help them remember details, do mathematical calculations and organize information. Computers also allow people to extend the capacities of their minds.

Like the car, a computer will provide many conveniences for those who are willing to learn to drive. However, using a computer is actually much safer than driving a car—crashing a hard drive and losing some data is certainly not as dangerous, or as expensive, as having an accident with your car.

So, are you ready to drive? Then hop aboard because computers will take us on our journey to the future.

What Computers Can Do for You

Why should we jump in and learn to use computers now? To put it in more common terms, what's in it for me? The answer to that question is . . . . Plenty!

The computer is an extension of your mind. As such, it can perform one very important function—it can make you look and feel smarter. Imagine how great you would feel handing your boss a professional report, complete with graphs and wonderfully formatted text! Imagine how great you would feel if the beautiful flyer that you created helped you sell a house! That would certainly make your customers think of you more professionally. Imagine how great you would feel if you could help your child turn in an outstanding homework assignment! It would be a great feeling for your kids to think that you could just possibly be smarter than they are. Yes, the computer can help you look and feel smarter both professionally and personally.

Just think how good you will feel when you are well-organized. Wouldn't you like to be able to remember the birthdays of all your friends and relatives and to be notified a few days in advance of the occasion so you could buy a card? Wouldn't you like to remember the names of your clients' spouses and children? Your brain can't handle all of that, but your computer can. It can help you organize your finances, your taxes, your family records, and all those little scraps of important information.

Oh, yes . . . a computer can do one other very important thing for you. It can help you to have more fun.

Helping you to enjoy life is one of the things that the computer does very, very well. It doesn't matter what your hobby is; there are software programs for just about every pastime. If you are an aviator, or would-be aviator, you can fly to Paris and land at the Orly airport without ever leaving your den. If you are an art lover, you can tour the most famous museums and see the world's greatest art treasures right on your computer screen. If you are a golfer, you can play Pebble Beach in the morning and Pinehurst #2 in the afternoon. You can even make new friends around the world, and find others with whom you can share your knowledge and enthusiasm about the things you love.

The History of Computers

First, we'll start with a brief history of the computer. Then we'll learn how the computer works.

Most people can give you a brief history of the automobile. They probably don't know how the engine works but at least they know where it is and what it looks like. That is our goal here—to give you a little background on computers so you can feel comfortable with them. Remember, the idea is not to memorize every word. Just sit back and enjoy; you will learn everything you need to know about computers.

If you were to take 100 people off the street and ask them who invented the computer, you would be lucky to find one person who knew the answer. But this is not a sign of ignorance. Many people contributed to the underlying technology of the computer. No one person was the sole inventor.

Actually, the precursor of the computer was the adding machine, invented by Blaise Pascal, a brilliant French mathematician and physicist. In 1642, Pascal decided to make his father's job at a local tax office easier. The result was a simple mechanical adding machine. There were some improvements to the adding machine over the years, but it was not until 1822 that an Englishman, Charles Babbage, created a computer-like machine. Babbage was a mathematician who used adding and subtracting mechanisms to create a machine that was able to do more complex mathematical calculations. These two inventions, along with other ideas and innovations, led to the creation of the computer.

Although there is still some debate on the subject, the first useful computer was presented to the public on February 14,

1946. It was called the ENIAC—an acronym for Electronic Numerical Integrator and Computer. You will notice that this was also the start of long and complex names given to computers and computer-related items, and then using alphabetical acronyms to represent them.

TIP
There is a glossary in the back of this book to help you with any computer terminology that you do not understand.

Two researchers, John Eckert and John Mauchly developed the ENIAC machine. They were awarded an Army contract in 1943 to calculate firing trajectories for artillery shells. The ENIAC machine housed 18,000 vacuum tubes and miles and miles of wiring. It weighed over 30 tons and was 18 feet high and 80 feet long. At the time, it was a marvel of technology. By today's standards ENIAC was a dinosaur, very large and very slow. Desktop computers today have over 1,000 times the ENIAC's processing power and several million times the capacity to store data.

Eckert and Mauchly formed their own company and transformed the nature of computer technology, but never became rich from their efforts. They ran out of money, and sold their company to Remington Rand. Ironically, they passed up an offer by Thomas Watson, Sr. to join IBM, which could have

changed their destiny dramatically. Remington Rand developed the Univac computer. IBM developed successful mainframe computers and eventually developed the personal computer.

"The farther backward you can look, the farther forward you are likely to see."

— Winston Churchill

One thing that becomes evident from this brief history of computers is a cyclical process moving from simplicity to complexity and then back to simplicity again. The technology starts with one simple invention, in this case the adding machine. Then it becomes more complex, as in the machines from the ENIAC to the mainframe computers. Then, that technology is somehow simplified. In this case, the invention of the silicon chip allowed for a smaller and simpler machine that was much more powerful.

Right now we are again in a simplification phase of the cycle. Personal computers are becoming simpler, faster and more "user friendly." Operating systems such as Windows have made computers easier to use. Computer companies are creating industry standards to help implement the hardware and software. This means that a certain type of CD-ROM drive or a certain type of adapter card becomes the industry standard. Remember the battle between VHS and Beta formats when videocassette recorders were first introduced? This simplification of the computer industry will take several more years, but will result in great benefits to computer users.

You may be thinking that even with all this "user-friendly" stuff, computers are still difficult to use. The goal of Compu-KISS is to help you realize that using computers can be both fun and easy to use. By the end of this book, you will see how lucky we are to be a part of the computer world at this particular point in history.

What a Computer Is and How It Works

Everyone knows what a computer is. How many of us, however, know how a computer works?

We normally work in the decimal numbering system. The word *decimal* denotes the number ten. In the decimal system there are ten numbers, from zero to nine. All our numbers are represented by some combination of these ten numbers.

The computer uses a different numbering system, the binary numbering system. Binary means two. Ones and zeros are the only numbers used in the binary system.

In its simplest state, a computer is just a series of on-off switches. If an electrical charge is present, that charge produces an "on" switch represented by the number 1. The lack of an electrical charge produces an "off" switch represented by the number 0. Strings of ones and zeros are linked together to represent numbers and letters. Every digital computer, no matter what its size or use, gets its instructions from this chain of information expressed as ones and zeros.

All the numbers, and even alphabetical characters, are represented by specific combinations of ones and zeros. For example 01000001 represents the letter A, and 01000010 represents the letter B. Each digit is called a *binary digit* or a *bit*. The string of eight bits or eight binary digits is called a *byte*.

This might seem like useless information to you. However, it is important to understand how a computer recognizes information. Once, I received a telephone call from a friend who was trying to give the computer the simple command "out." He had been typing the word "out" over and over again, but the computer did not respond. After asking him a few questions, I determined that, being new to the keyboard world, he had accidentally used the "zero" key instead of the "O" key when he typed the word "out." The binary representation of the letter "O" is 01001111. The binary representation of the number "zero" is 00110000. As you can see, these two digits are very different in the computer's language. The computer did not recognize what he wanted because he was giving it the wrong command.

Sometimes the computer expects a space in a certain location when you enter data. A space has its own binary code or *byte*. If the computer does not find a space in the correct location, it will not respond correctly. This has caused frustration for many computer users. You see, the computer is not trying to work against you. You simply need to give the computer the correct information.

Hardware and Software

When speaking of computers, two terms are commonly used: *hardware* and *software*. Hardware is anything that pertains to the physical components or the equipment that makes up a computer system. The computer monitor, modem and printer would all be types of computer hardware. In contrast, the programs or instructions that tell the computer what to do is called software. Software includes any programs that you purchase, as well as those that come with the computer. A word processing program such as WordPerfect would be a type of computer software. An *operating system*, such as Windows, is also a type of software. The operating system is the software that controls all of the basic computer functions. It is composed of thousands of instructions that tell the computer hardware how to function.

A Summary . . .

1. *You are already part of the computer revolution.*

2. *Computers are an extension of your mind.*

3. *Computers can make your life easier.*

4. *Computers think in simple binary language consisting of 1s and 0s.*

5. *Computers use both hardware and software.*

Buying a New Computer

———◆———

Chapter 2

"The only thing more expensive than education is ignorance."

— Benjamin Franklin

Today's technology is moving at such a rapid pace that the computer you buy today is outdated quickly. You need to understand exactly what you are purchasing to invest your computer dollars wisely.

Purchasing a computer can be an intimidating task for almost anyone. Even a fast-talking car salesperson can look mild compared to a fast-talking computer salesperson. The trick here is to do your homework *before* you buy. Decide what type of work and what fun things you would like to do with your computer. I'll give you some ideas later in this book. Go shopping and look at software, or read mail-order catalogues to see what type of software is available.

Read through the next few sections of this book and make a list of all the things you need in a computer. Remember that to be a confident computer shopper, you must be well-informed.

My current recommendation is to buy a computer with a Pentium 166 to 200 MHz processor, with 16-32 megabytes of RAM, a one or two gigabyte hard disk, an 8- or 12-speed CD-

ROM, a local bus video card with 1 or 2 megabytes of RAM, a 15" or 17" monitor with at least .28 dot pitch resolution, a 16-bit sound card and speakers. Windows 95 should come pre-installed. Hopefully other software will also come with the computer.

Now we are finally there, into the nitty-gritty, real hard core computer language. Don't worry though. By the time you go into the computer store, you'll know what you're talking about. Read on.

If you are not purchasing a computer right now, that's okay, too. Just think how much better you will feel at the next party you attend when the conversation turns to computers and you are able to participate intelligently.

Now, let's look at the computer step-by-step. I will explain each part of the computer separately. Then, I will give you a brief look at what the future of each component might be. This information will help you make your purchase, as well as understand where the computer world is headed.

Operating Systems

The operating system is essentially the software that runs the computer. It also allows you to interact with the computer. As such, it is an important part of the computer.

UNIX and DOS

There are two older operating systems that are still in use today: UNIX and DOS. You will probably not purchase a new computer which uses either program as its main operating system. However, these two systems are still widely used in businesses and large mainframe computers, as well as in many of the

computers that make up the Internet. In fact, Windows 3.1 and Windows 95 both use DOS as an underlying basis to their operating systems.

Older operating systems such as UNIX and DOS are character-based and not very graphic or intuitive. Working with them requires you to learn to speak "their special language."

Choosing an Operating System

One of the major decisions regarding the purchase of a personal computer is whether you should buy an IBM-compatible computer or a Macintosh (Mac) made by Apple Computers and several other companies that make Mac clones. The reason this is a major decision is that the two computers each run different operating systems and are generally incompatible. Hardware and software have recently been developed that moves the two types of computers closer together. However, the decision should be relatively easy for you.

The vast majority—over 90%—of PCs sold today are IBM-compatible. Because of this, there is much more software available for an IBM-compatible than there is for the Mac. That alone is a valid reason to buy the IBM-compatible. The introduction of Windows 95 has eliminated the question of "ease of use" between the two types of computers. Windows 95 mimics the Macintosh operating system and is almost as user-friendly. I believe that the Mac is still a little easier to use, but the differences now are minor.

If you have decided to buy a Mac, you will receive the current version of the Macintosh operating system on your machine. Most new IBM-compatible machines today are shipped with Windows 95 pre-installed on the hard disk. Both of these are excellent operating systems.

The newer Windows-based systems are much easier and more user-friendly. If you are using Windows 3.1, consider upgrading to Windows 95. You might need to upgrade your hardware, and will definitely want to upgrade your software, but in most cases, it is worth the investment.

IBM also has its own operating system called OS2. This is a very good operating system of the same type and level as Windows 95. The problem is that IBM has not been able to break into the mass market with OS2, so there is much more software available for Windows 95.

The last operating system to mention is called Windows NT. It is an excellent and a very stable Windows-based operating system, yet carries a high price and large memory requirements. It is used mainly for medium-to-large business operations.

We can assume that Windows-based systems will remain the operating systems of choice for the near future. I expect that one of the next versions of Windows will merge Windows NT with Windows 95. If Microsoft, the developer of Windows, incorporates some rich, new features into their next version of Windows, it could turn out to be a dynamic operating system. However, the better the operating system, the more hardware resources it will require. So expect to see the need for more memory and bigger hard disks in desktop machines. Don't worry though—prices should continue to drop so that we can all afford the things that we need.

Apple—Should You Take a Bite?

Apple is preparing a new generation of computers with an entirely new operating system. If they live up to their expectations, they may create a resurgence in Apple computers. In the mean time, in my opinion there remain only a few solid reasons for buying a Mac.

First, the major reason for

purchasing a Mac is to be compatible with the type of computer you use at work, or that you or another family member uses at school. If you will be taking files back and forth between work or school and home and you use a Mac at work or school, then you should buy a Mac.

Second, you will find that many public schools use Macintosh computers. However, if your children use a Mac at school, you can still buy an IBM-compatible for home use. You can purchase similar programs for your home computer and children will usually adapt to using both systems with no major problems.

Third, Mac computers have a stronghold in the world of graphic art and design. The IBM-compatibles are now almost as powerful as the Macs for the chores of the graphic artist, but many newspapers, publishers, etc. still use Macs. If you need a computer for specific graphic work, decide which software you need and base your decision on that.

"Thinking is hard work."

— Thomas Alva Edison

Central Processing Unit

The computer's main component is called the Central Processing Unit, or CPU for short. The CPU is the brain of the computer, equivalent to the engine of a car. It interacts with all the other parts of the computer. The faster the CPU, the faster the whole computer. As you know, relays or vacuum tubes ran the first computers. Then in the late 1940s the transistor was developed. This was a gigantic breakthrough for all electrical equipment. Transistors allow electrical impulses to be transmitted as on-off switches, without mechanical movement. This allowed for much smaller components. Transistors today, serve as the nerve cells of the computer.

The biggest compression of the computer processor came in the late 1950s with the discovery of the integrated circuit, or "chip" for short. The integrated circuit is simply a semiconductor piece of material, such as silicon, with the transistors and other electrical components, such as capacitors and resistors, built into the same piece of material. Today, the CPU of a computer is a tiny piece of silicon, which is also referred to as the silicon chip or the processor chip. Interestingly, the silicon for a computer chip is refined from ordinary sand.

The CPU resides in the computer on what's called the *motherboard*, the main circuit board of the computer.

The CPU chips originally had numerical names. You might hear an older CPU referred to as an *80286* or an *80386*. After awhile, the "80" part was generally dropped and the CPUs were simply called *286*, *386* or *486*. Each of these refers to a family of CPUs and indicates sequence of development. Each family of CPUs improved upon its predecessor, so the *486* is faster and better than the *386*. When the *586* was put into production, Intel, the mother-of-all chip manufacturers, decided to give the processor chips more common names. So they called the *586*, the *Pentium* chip. The *686*, is called the *Pentium II*.

You might see a chip by a manufacturer other than Intel called a *586*. This would be roughly comparable to the Pentium chip, but typically requires a higher processor speed to achieve the same performance as a Pentium chip. For example: a 586-133 MHz is roughly equivalent to a Pentium-75 MHz in performance.

Another variation of the Pentium chip is the MMX, which adds multimedia extensions to the computer chip. This gives the chip enhancements in the area of media processing functions such as video, 3-D and sound. With MMX, you are able to view video on a full screen instead of in a little window. You can also view items on the computer screen in a more natural, three-dimensional way. MMX chips make speech recognition better, improve video conferencing and can significantly improve presentations. Only software that is written specifically for MMX chips is able to take advantage of these features. Games written for the MMX chip produce much more realistic and exciting new worlds for the game buff.

Intel works diligently to try to convince the computer consumer that its chips are superior to other brands. However, based on independent testing, chips by most other manufacturers are comparable in speed and accuracy. It is like buying a generic product at the grocery store. The generic product often offers comparable quality to the name-brand equivalent. However, if you want to be assured of constant quality, you will choose the name-brand product.

While Intel produces most of the chips for IBM-compatible personal computers, Motorola produces most of the chips for the Apple and Macintosh-type computers. If you are looking in that market, you should be shopping for a 100 MHz PowerPC chip, if at all possible. These chips are the Motorola equivalent to the Pentium chip and actually have the potential to be faster than the Pentium. Unfortunately, they perform to their potential only when running software written specifically for the Power PC chip. At the present time, there is not much software of that type on the market.

Processor Speeds

The second important feature in processor chips is the speed of the processor's internal clock. These clock speeds are measured in millions of cycles per second or megahertz (MHz).

The megahertz usually ranges from 25 to over 200, with faster chips being introduced everyday.

Clock speeds are relatively easy to understand. The higher the megahertz, the faster the computing speed. In computing, speed doesn't just equate to power, it also equates to time. A slow computer will make you wait while a screen redraws, or while it computes data. This is usually only a matter of a few seconds of waiting time. However, if you use your computer for several hours each day, those few seconds of waiting time can become frustrating. You can sometimes upgrade the processor chip of your computer later, but this is often fairly complicated and expensive. It is better to purchase the fastest CPU that you can afford.

Faster and Faster

As the technology used in producing processor chips continues to improve daily, the chips get faster and faster. When that happens, the other components of the computer also have  to be updated to take advantage of the processor speeds. Certainly, new and better chips will be introduced on a continuing basis—that is the nature of the industry. The 486 chip is still a viable processor for running today's software, as it has been for several years, although its life span is nearly over. The Pentium and Pentium Pro will likely have a life at least as long as the 486 and is the better choice today.

Memory

The built-in memory of a computer is called RAM, for Random Access Memory. You can think of this type of memory as the size of the top of your desk. The more room that you have on your desk, the more projects you can work on at the same time. This type of memory is cleared when you turn the computer off; it is only a temporary storage place. If you have an adequate amount of RAM you can run several programs at one time, and you can also run large programs. As the programs and operating systems get bigger, PCs need more and more RAM. RAM is measured in megabytes (MB). "More is better" applies here, too. Pentiums or PowerMacs will usually run on 4 megabytes of memory, but really need 8 megabytes to run smoothly. Going up to 16 megabytes, is especially beneficial for multimedia applications. Your entire system will run much faster and more smoothly with 16 MB. You will need to add more memory if you run any specialized software such as Windows NT or Auto Cad, or any other program that requires complex mathematical calculations. If you can afford to buy 16 or 32 MB now, do it. In the future if you need more memory, it can be added easily.

Hard Disk Storage

The hard disk is a platter with a magnetic coating. This platter or disk is the place where you can permanently store your files. Any discussion about hard disks can be summed up in three words. Bigger is better! I recommend that you get at least a one-gigabyte (1 GB) hard disk. It sounds like a lot of hard disk, but believe me, it will probably fill up before you know it.

You will find that most people use the words *hard disk* and *hard drive* interchangeably. The drive is really the mechanism that controls the hard disk. The disk is the part of the mechanism that holds the data files, programs and other information.

Most hard drives today are quite fast. The speed of a hard drive is measured in *access time*. That is the amount of time that the hard drive needs to find your information. It is usually measured in milliseconds. A seek time of 12 milliseconds is adequate for most applications. If you want to compare access times, remember that the shorter the access time, the faster the hard drive.

Will hard disks just keep getting bigger? The answer is yes. As software offers more and better features, it will take up more room on the hard disk. So the computer user will need bigger hard disks. There are several new technologies being developed that will make larger storage disks available. A new technology called Near-field recording (NFR), which uses optical technology, promises to offer ten times the capacity of hard disks at comparable speeds and costs.

As the Internet continues to grow, it may become the mainstream method of computing. Perhaps, in the future, all our programs and operating systems will be stored at some central location on the Internet. If that happens, we will need a hard disk only to store our personal data files. Until that time, however, buy as big a hard disk as you can afford.

Monitors

Monitors come in various sizes. The most common are 14", 15" and 17", measured diagonally across the face of the tube. If you have ever worked on a 17" monitor, you will never want to go back to using a 14" or 15" monitor again. A 15" monitor is adequate for most applications. If you can afford a monitor that is 17" or larger, it's a great investment.

The monitor's resolution is the amount of detail that it can display. Most monitors today are called Super VGA. These can show more detail than the older VGA monitors. There are two types of monitors: *interlaced* and *non-interlaced*. You will find that interlaced monitors are cheaper, but the quality of the display suffers. They will usually have a slight flickering that is not good for your eyes. You will definitely want to spend a little more and purchase a non-interlaced monitor.

Most monitors stipulate a certain dot pitch. The dot pitch is really the spacing between the dots of color on the screen. The smaller the pitch, the sharper the image and the less eyestrain you will encounter. My recommendation is to buy a monitor with .28 dot pitch or less.

I have already mentioned eye strain several times in reference to monitors. Even if you only use the computer occasionally, you want to protect your eyes. So be sure to buy a good monitor.

There has also been extensive publicity regarding monitors and electromagnetic radiation. This should be a concern when buying and using a computer. Obviously, the more time you spend in front of the computer, the more you should be concerned with levels of radiation. There are two things you can do to protect yourself. First, keep the monitor 24" to 36" away from your body. Second, make sure that the monitor has passed some level of emission testing. The actual results of such testing are quite complicated. Sweden has set a good standard for these tests. If you want to be sure that you are protected, just make sure that the  monitor you buy or use is up to Swedish (MPR II) standards. Again, you will pay a little more for a low-emission monitor, but it will be a wise investment.

It will probably be years before we know how harmful the emissions from computer monitors really are, but in the meantime, better to be safe than sorry!

Ask questions when you purchase a computer system. The monitor is where many dealers skimp. They will often give you a good computer system with a poor monitor. Other times you will think that the price includes everything, only to find out later that the monitor is priced separately. Buyers beware!

The industry should see a significant improvement in monitors, because the technology for making larger, flat screen monitors is already in place. When they do make their appearance on your desk top, the difference will be dramatic.

Video Boards

Inside the computer there is a mechanism that processes video information and transforms it into shapes and pictures on your monitor screen. In a personal computer, that mechanism is called the video board. The video board, or card, determines how well your computer display works, especially when displaying graphics or pictures. It has its own memory. One or two megabytes of video memory are adequate. But if you work with photos or other graphics in your computing, you should have at least four megabytes of video memory.

There are two types of memory involved in video memory: *DRAM* (Dynamic RAM) and *VRAM* (Video RAM). If you will be using multimedia applications, the VRAM will make video playback much smoother. If you want to have TV-quality video you must buy a video board with full-motion video. The main problem with full-motion video is that an ordinary video board cannot handle all the video information. The information needs to be compressed and decompressed as it is transferred. The best scheme for doing that right now is called *MPEG*, named after the Motion Pictures Expert Group.

Another consideration when you buy a video board is the type of *bus* system that the computer uses. If you think of transportation when you think of a bus system, you are right. The bus is the connection between the CPU and the video board along which all information travels. To avoid that frustration, get what is known as a *local bus*. The design of the local bus overcomes the speed limitations imposed by older bus designs. A local bus works at the speed of the CPU. That means the local bus can take full advantage of a fast CPU. That is exactly what you need to speed up the video on your computer.

PCI, which stands for *Peripheral Component Interconnect*, is the local bus standard in most PCs today.

Full-motion video will probably be improved as computers begin to deliver the picture quality that we have come to expect from television.

CD-ROM

CD-ROMs have become an integral part of computer systems. A CD-ROM can play music compact disks on your computer and more importantly, it can give you access to multimedia software. A compact disk can contain much more information than the older floppy disks. In fact, the entire contents of an encyclopedia, along with sound and video clips, can be stored on one disk. As with other computer technology, it is rapidly improving. The current standard is called *8-X* or eight speed, although *12-X* and even faster CD-ROM players are available. A good 8-speed CD-ROM is adequate. If your new system comes with a higher speed drive, that's great.

Remember that the faster your equipment is, the longer it will last before it becomes obsolete.

There are also CD-ROM disk changers on the market that hold more than one disk, just like audio compact disk changers. Once you begin using your CDs frequently you will get tired of putting them in and out of the computer and will wish that you had one of these.

Most CD-ROMs on the market are photo-compatible. That means that you can have your photos developed on a CD-ROM and display them on your computer. You can then use your computer to correct mistakes, such as red eyes. You can also improve the quality of your pictures with software tools. Digital cameras have become available at affordable prices. As this technology improves it will become very powerful.

Right now, most CD-ROMs are *read only*. ROM stands for "read only memory." That means that you cannot save a file on a compact disk. A special disk player with recording capabilities will produce a *CD-R* (CD-rewritable). There are also *CD-E* (CD-erasable) disks and drives that will allow you to write to a CD and erase what you have written and rewrite something else on that disc, just as you do now with a floppy disk.

Another new technology is DVD, Digital Video Disk. These disks will hold much more information than the current CDs. DVDs can store a full-length movie on one disk. This technology will help to mesh television with computers.

"A good listener is not only popular everywhere, but after a while he knows something."

— *Wilson Mizner*

Sound Cards

The *sound card*, or *soundboard* in your computer allows you to hook speakers up to the computer and have the computer produce sound. The sound card also translates the sound track on a CD-ROM disk into a sound signal for loudspeakers. The most common sound card on the market, the 16-bit Sound Blaster-compatible card, is the industry standard for audio cards. It will give you adequate sound for most applications. A 32-bit sound card will give you better sound than a 16-bit card.

There are also more advanced cards that allow you to clearly hear several sounds or instruments at the same time. These cards are called *wave tables*. You will want to consider one of these if you plan to hook up a keyboard or guitar to your computer system.

Some computers come with built-in speakers and a built-in microphone. For most computers though, you will need a set of speakers to hook up to your sound card. Most computer speakers are magnetically shielded so they don't interfere with the electronic mechanism of the computer. Also, most computers need amplified speakers, which have their own power source. You can hook up regular speakers to your computer through an amplifier, however it is usually easier to purchase a set of self-powered computer speakers.

Although most computers come with speakers, very few have built-in microphones or come with a microphone. You will need a microphone if you plan to give your computer voice commands, if you plan to use your computer to study a foreign language, or if you want to use your computer for telephone answering-machine functions.

If you need to purchase a microphone, look at the back of the computer and find the spot where you will hook in the microphone. It is usually on the sound card and marked "in" or "mic." You will now be able to see the correct size of the plug you need to purchase for the microphone. Most standard microphones with the right-size adapter should work.

There are a couple of items worth considering when you buy a sound card. A *subwoofer* boosts the bass and can add dimension to your system's sound. New 3-D sound card/speaker systems can envelop you in sound. Granted, these are extra luxuries for most computer users, but they can be fun.

With all the other technological improvements, the quality of sound for the computer has not improved greatly. The next buzz word in this area will be *voice recognition*. With voice recognition your computer will be able to recognize the sound of your voice and will be able to initiate commands and/or take dictation without the use of the keyboard or mouse. There has been considerable research in this field. The voice recognition software available now is a great improvement over previous attempts. Eventually, all computers will understand all voices and respond to these voices, just as they do on Star Trek.

Floppy Disks

When the personal computer made its debut, information was transferred in and out of the computer on a square 5¼" soft-sided diskette, which became known as a floppy disk. That disk has now been replaced by a hard plastic 3½" diskette. Although the 3½" diskette is hard, it is still known as a floppy disk. Most PCs today come with a 3½" disk drive built in. This is still a convenient way to move files from one computer to another.

You can buy floppy disks, pre-formatted for either IBM or Mac. If they are not pre-formatted, you will have to format them yourself. Formatting a disk is an easy, yet somewhat time-consuming process. Go to the operating system of your computer (i.e. Windows 95 or Windows 3.1) and type in "format floppy" for simple instructions on how to format a floppy.

As the size of software programs increase, floppy disks become harder to work with because they hold only a limited amount of information. Today a program may come on ten or twenty floppy disks. That is one of the reasons that CD-ROMs have become so popular. You can install a program from one CD-ROM without having to feed numerous floppies into the computer.

Until CD-Rs (rewritable CD-ROMs) become more commonplace, you will need a place for temporary storage of files. You need a removable disk or cartridge which you can write to and erase at your convenience. Some other type of improved storage will eventually replace floppy disks. Right now there are a myriad of such drives on the market. All work quite well, however, none of them have become the obvious successor to the floppy drive.

TIP

Floppy disks that are used frequently need to be replaced because disk wear can cause a disk to malfunction.

Mass Storage Units

There are several options for storing data when you need more storage space than a floppy drive provides.

Very high-capacity diskettes and cartridges are available. They are roughly the size of 3½" floppies, but are often thicker. These disks require a special drive. They allow for storage of

100 MB or more on a single disk. They have good access times and can even be used like an additional hard disk. Iomega is one of the main suppliers of these disk drives. Iomega's drives are called *Zip drives* or *Jaz drives.* Other companies such as SyQuest also market good high-capacity drives. All of these drives are good for storage of large data files and for back-up purposes.

These drives are often called removable drives. Most can be installed in an empty bay in your computer, but they can also be purchased as a freestanding unit and used as a removable device. If attached in this manner, they can be used for many purposes. They can provide backup for computers in more than one location. One drive can also be used to transport files from one computer to another.

If you plan to use one of these drives to transfer large files to another computer, find out which drive the other computer uses, because these drives are not all compatible.

Tape drives are available for storing large amounts of data. They are the cheapest mass storage units available. Tape drives are generally used only for back-up purposes because they provide somewhat slow access times.

Keyboards

The keyboard is an integral part of the computer. A standard version is often included when you purchase a computer. These keyboards are adequate, but if you type information into the computer for more than an hour at a time, try one of the newer *ergonomic* keyboards. These keyboards are specially designed to help prevent repetitive stress injuries. There are also some keyboards available that have special programmable keys. These are useful if you type in a foreign language, which requires letters that we do not have in our alphabet. Also, some companies are offering keyboards with special keys for Windows 95. This is a nice feature if you are working in that operating system.

Actually, the biggest difference in keyboards is the tactile feel of the keys. Some people like to have the keys click when they press them, others prefer a more mushy feel. If you have a choice of keyboards, test-drive them to see if you like the way they feel.

The keyboard is often one of the first components of the computer to wear out. With heavy use, it is not unusual for a keyboard to have to be replaced on a yearly basis. So if you don't like your keyboard, purchase another one. Then keep the original keyboard as a spare.

"You see things, and you say "Why?";
but I dream things that never were,
and I say: Why not?"

— George Bernard Shaw

Mouse

The other input device, in common use with computers today, is the mouse. Many people seem to be curious about how the mouse got its name. In the late 1950s and early 1960s a man named Douglas Engelbart became fascinated with a theory that he called "human augmentation technology"—that is, the idea that computers should be used to enhance human performance. Up to that time, computers were thought of as being useful only to the military and scientific communities. Engelbart was laughed at and rejected by the computer science community, yet his ideas were precursors for today's personal computers. He foresaw the use of the computer as a word processor and much, much more. In 1968, he made an input device to help people interact with the

41

computer. Since it was small and had a tail-like cord hanging from it, he called it a mouse. Englebart's ideas were rejected, only to be later resurrected by others who took the credit and financial rewards for his ideas. The mouse was one of his most ingenious ideas. The mouse that we use today has changed little since Englebart's days.

There is a difference, however, between a good mouse and a cheap mouse. A good mouse will have a more contoured shape and feel more comfortable in your hand. It will also behave better on the screen. It will be more responsive. Some people have large hands. Some have small hands. For this reason, choosing a mouse is a personal thing. If at all possible, try out the mouse before you buy it. If you get a cheap one with your computer, replace it with something you like.

When shopping for a mouse, you will notice that most have two buttons, but a few have three buttons. The left mouse button is commonly used with most applications. The right mouse button is also used with newer software for providing an extra menu of choices. In some programs you can use the third mouse button to scroll down the screen. This comes in handy in many instances. For example, when on the Internet, you often see only half of the page at one time. A three-button mouse allows you to easily see the whole page without having to move your mouse around. This is a useful feature for those who spend a lot of time on the Internet.

> **TIP**
>
> Your computer can also act like an answering machine to answer your telephone calls. To do this, you need a modem with voice capabilities, also called a *voice modem.*

Modems

The future of communications, as it relates to computers, is boundless. As we are now in the midst of major changes in the world of communications, telephone, cable and communication companies are all jockeying for position, hoping to become the profit leader. Eventually, we will probably use either ISDN-type telephone lines (digital computer lines), cable television lines or satellites for our computer communications.

A modem is the device computers use to communicate over the telephone lines. For two computers in different locations to communicate, they must both be equipped with modems. Modem speeds are measured in bits-per-second, (Bps). These are the number of symbol elements or *bits* transmitted each second. Currently, modem speeds range from 2,400 Bps to 56,000 Bps. You will also see modem speeds listed in kilobits per second (Kbps). A modem that is listed as 28,800 Bps and 28.8Kbps is the same. The higher the number, the faster the modem. Faster is better.

The best computers will augment the modem with fax capabilities. This is called a fax-modem. These useful devices combined with a scanner, are the equivalent of a free-standing fax machine.

Buy the fastest communication device that you can afford. Even so, you will find that it is not fast enough. Anyone who has waited while the computer transferred a large file knows that communication devices and transmission lines need to be faster. We don't like to sit around and wait.

There are exceptionally fast modems that use special telephone lines called Integrated Services Digital Network or *ISDN* lines. These lines allow more information to be transmitted faster, and they also allow for information to travel in both directions at the same time. Since they are capable of handling both data and voice transmissions, video conferencing and other telephone-like communications can be accomplished through the computer. Right now ISDN lines are quite expensive and may not be readily available outside of large metro-politan areas.

There are also special modems, DSVD (Digital Simultaneous Voice and Data), which allow for data and sound to be transmitted at one time over telephone lines. Both users must have DSVD modems for this technology to work.

Basically, there are two types of modems: internal and external. Internal modems are on computer boards or cards like the video card and they reside inside the computer. External modems are about the size of your hand. They attach to the computer with a wire and sit on your desktop. So which one should you buy? If you are purchasing a new computer, get an internal modem. It will be installed, configured and ready to run when you get the computer home. If you are adding a modem to an existing computer, spend a few extra dollars and get an external modem. It is not worth opening up the computer and installing a board when you can buy something that you simply plug in. Both the internal and external modems are identical in the way they work, once they are installed.

For now, buy the fastest modem you can. Jump in. You'll enjoy communicating with the rest of the world on your computer.

Ports

The *port* is the connection between your computer and another device on your system. It allows information to flow in and out of the computer. There are two main types of ports: the *serial port* and the *parallel port*. The parallel port is usually used to attach a printer. The serial port is used to attach a modem or a mouse. Some printers can also use a serial port, but they will work more slowly. The typical computer has one parallel port and two serial ports. That is usually adequate unless you know that you will be using extra printers or other peripherals (A peripheral is any external device that connects to a computer).

USB (Universal Serial Bus) is a port that allows users to plug in a peripheral and have it automatically configured and ready to use. USB ports make adding equipment to your computer easy, but not all computer equipment is compatible with USB. If you have the option of purchasing a USB port on your new computer it is a good idea to include it. This will make adding new components easier in the future.

Expansion Slots and Bays

Expansion slots are areas inside the computer which are reserved for adding additional computer boards. You may not feel that you will need to add anything to your computer, but you probably will. Next month you may decide that you want to watch TV in the corner of your computer screen while you write your thesis. That would require you to install an additional board in your computer. Next year, you may want to add another computer device. You will want to have one or two open slots so that you can add additional boards to your computer, as needed.

Your computer should also have at least one extra *bay*. A bay is an area where you can install a larger computer device, such as a CD-ROM or tape back-up. Again, even if you don't plan to add anything, it's a good idea to have at least one free drive bay.

Cache and BIOS

There are two other computer terms that you will hear when you go to the computer store. They are *cache* (pronounced like the word cash) and *BIOS* (pronounced Bye-ous).

The cache helps to move data between the main memory and the processor with the least delay. Without a cache, the processor may sit idle while it waits for information to be passed to it. In other words, a cache makes the computer work faster. A cache typically consists of between 64 to 512 kilobytes of memory. Again, the bigger, the better.

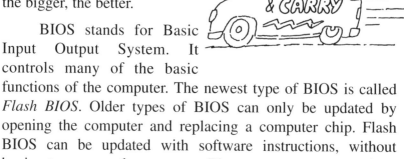

BIOS stands for Basic Input Output System. It controls many of the basic functions of the computer. The newest type of BIOS is called *Flash BIOS*. Older types of BIOS can only be updated by opening the computer and replacing a computer chip. Flash BIOS can be updated with software instructions, without having to open up the computer. There are not many occasions when you need to update the BIOS on your computer, but if you ever needed to do it, the flash BIOS would obviously be easier to manage.

Bundled Software

When you are shopping for a new computer you are often offered bundled software as an incentive to buy. This is software that comes with your computer at no extra charge. Computer companies purchase software directly from the manufacturer and then install it on your computer. It is usually ready to run when you get it home. This is a great way to get software. The value, however, is sometimes questionable.

The first thing to consider is the usefulness of the software. If they are offering you ten children's software programs and you have no children to use them, then you are getting no added value. If, however, you are a parent of young children, that software might be important to you. So, first consider whether or not you will actually use the software. Second, consider how much the software is actually worth. Go to the software store, or get a mail-order catalog, and add up the price that you would pay if you bought the software separately. That way you will know exactly what the software add-on is really worth. You should also make sure that the software being offered is current. Some companies will bundle last year's versions. This practice seems to be used especially in the CD-ROM software, such as reference pieces. Do you really want a CD that has a complete collection of TIME magazines from three years ago? Or an atlas that still shows the Soviet Union intact? If the software is new, it may be an enticement to buy, otherwise it may mean nothing.

Another hook that computer manufacturers are using is free on-line time and free software to CompuServe, America Online or other on-line services. This is not a bargain. All the on-line services will give free software and free time on-line to anyone interested in subscribing to their services.

A Summary . . .

1. Operating Systems are the source of your computer's thoughts.

2. The central processing unit (CPU) is your computer's brain.

3. Memory (RAM) is the computer's working memory.

4. The hard disk is the container that holds copies of your files and programs.

5. The monitor is the visual presentation of your data.

Being a Smart Computer Shopper

◆

Chapter 3

"Styling and value are what sells cars, but quality is what keeps them sold."

— *Lee Iacocca*

Cars and computers have many similarities. Styling and value are important considerations when purchasing either item. Quality, however, is the lasting characteristic. This is what makes the brand of computer that you purchase one of the most important decisions that you will make.

Choosing a Computer Company

The information that we have given so far will enable you to make an informed decision about the computer you want to buy and what components should be included. By this time you have probably looked around and you may have a good idea of how much money you will have to spend to get the computer that fits your needs. One major decision remains—which company should you purchase your computer from? As with any mechanical device, the key word is *reliability*. If you compare computers to cars you will find that the computer, in general, is much more reliable. As you know, certain car manufacturers have a reputation for better quality and reliability. The same is true for computer manufacturers.

There is one big difference between cars and computers when you look at them for reliability. In the automotive world, there are a specific number of manufacturers and each manufacturer puts out only a few car models each year. That is not true for computers. First, there are many more computer manufacturers. Each company continually updates their models as the year goes on. That means that the number of available models of computers may become confusing.

"Before you invest—investigate."

— Salmon P. Halle

Reliability Ratings

When you start to research computer companies, you can consult the *Consumer Reports* ratings on computers. However, *Consumer Reports* takes a specific manufacturer and a specific model with specific components and tries to rate that particular computer. Unless you are able to buy that exact computer with the identical specified equipment, you cannot be sure how good it is. A better way is to find out which company is the most reliable in general. Every year the major computer magazines review computer manufacturers. They include reliability ratings

as well as things like customer satisfaction—the amount of time it took to reach a representative by phone, and the amount of time it took to resolve the problem. *PC Magazine* and *PC World* are two of the major magazines that publish these ratings.

Warranties

When choosing a computer manufacturer, carefully examine the company's warranty policy. Many companies offer three-year warranties. It is certainly an advantage to know that the computer is covered by a long warranty, but the warranty is only as good as the company. What good is a three-year warranty if the company closes its doors next year? Most likely you will be looking at name brand computers that have a good reputation. If, however, you are looking at a company that you are unsure of, check out the company's stability by gathering as much information as you can. The Better Business Bureau in the region where the company is located can tell you how long the company has been in business and if they have ever been, or are now, in bankruptcy. The Better Business Bureau can also tell you if there have been any complaints against the company.

Technical Support

You also want to be sure that the company's technical support will be available when you need it. *Tech Support* is the department that you call when you have a technical question about your computer or the software that came with it. Try to determine how much you will be using tech support. If you have worked with computers before and are familiar with them, you might not use tech support very often. If you are new to computers, you can count on using tech support more frequently. When you have questions, tech support is the place to get those questions answered.

If you expect to use tech support frequently, look for a computer company that has a toll-free number. Even with the best of companies, there will be times when there are more calls than there are agents on duty. Those long distance charges will add up quickly when you are put on hold. Also, check out the hours that the companies' technical support lines are open. Some companies have 24-hour support. This is really great for night owls. It also helps to spread the calls out and usually results in better response times.

Mail-Order Buying

As you begin to investigate computer companies, you will find that some of them are mail-order companies. Don't automatically discount these. You will usually find some of these companies in the top-ten lists for reliability and service. When you call these companies you will probably find that the sales people on the phone are as knowledgeable as the ones in retail stores. The one drawback of mail-order is that you cannot try out the equipment to see if you like the keyboard and mouse and to get an idea of the speed of the machine. Most mail-order companies try to overcome that by offering you a 30-day-no-questions-asked return policy. You should always check out the return policy in detail.

Mail-order buying does have some advantages: 1) You can often find good prices from mail-order companies, and 2) Most important of all, mail-order allows you to customize your system easily. You can often pick and choose your components, add more memory, and change components to suit your needs. There are only a few retail stores that will do this for you.

If you buy by mail, there are a few things that you should keep in mind. The mail-order company is not necessarily the manufacturer. Some mail-order companies, such as IBM PC Direct, Dell and Gateway are linked directly to the manufacturer.

Other mail-order companies, such as Computer Discount Warehouse, PC Connection and MicroWarehouse are distributors who represent several different brands of equipment. If you are purchasing from a distributor, you must also check out both the mail-order company and the manufacturer. You will find that computer magazines write excellent reviews of mail-order companies. Always buy with a credit card. This gives you some recourse if something does go wrong.

When you order from a published ad, make sure that you save the ad for reference after you receive the computer. If you do not have anything written with the price, have the company fax or mail you a complete list of the equipment quoted and the price, including shipping and taxes. I learned this lesson the hard way. I ordered a computer from the company that was the number-one-rated manufacturer at that time. When I called, the representative told me about a new computer model they had just started shipping. He quoted me a great price. It sounded perfect. I ordered it and it was perfect. However, when the credit card bill came, it was $500 over the price quoted. I had no written proof of the quote. It took over five months and a letter to the president of the company and its board of directors to get things straightened out. So, learn from my mistake. Have written proof of the price.

Be sure to check out shipping charges too. Some companies charge a low flat rate. Others charge by weight, which can be substantial if you are purchasing a whole computer system. Also be aware that if you decide to return the computer, you may be responsible for paying the shipping charges in one or both directions.

A Summary . . .

1. *Purchase the computer that is right for you.*

2. *Know what you need before you start shopping.*

3. *Investigate the company that you will be buying from.*

4. *Know up front what the exact warranty is.*

5. *Get the details regarding the company's technical support policies.*

Setting Up Your Computer

———◆———

Chapter 4

"The greatest thing in the world is to know how to be self-sufficient."

— Montaigne

Now that you have bought the right computer at the right price, it's time to get it up and running. Unlike purchasing a car where you just fill up the tank, turn the key and go, there are several steps that you must take before you start up your computer.

Although there are several components and cables that come with your computer, setting it up is not a difficult task. If you don't feel comfortable doing it, hire someone to set it up for you. If you decide to do it yourself, you'll find it a fairly easy task.

First consider where you will put your computer. Finding room for a computer is not always easy. There are several things you need to know. It is preferable to keep the computer equipment out of the hot sun. The sun and/or any bright lights can cause an aggravating glare on the screen. You can buy anti-glare screens to put over the monitor screen, but it is easier to avoid the glare in the first place. Keep the computer away from heat sources and never place it in front of an air conditioner.

If you have bought a desktop computer, it will usually sit

on top of your desk with the monitor on top of it. A tower computer unit will usually sit on the floor, however it is actually preferable to have it on a sturdy table or desk where it will accumulate less dirt and dust.

Make sure that your computer has room to breath. All computers and monitors have vents. They need to have air circulating around them so they don't overheat. Try to keep at least a three-inch clearance around the air vents. Also, don't put things on top of the monitor if the monitor air vents are on top.

Make sure that you have an electrical outlet available. Also, if your computer has a modem, you will need to have a telephone jack available as well. If your computer will be using your main telephone line, you can buy a small adapter that will allow you to plug both the computer and the telephone into the same outlet.

Since monitor cables are usually fairly short, you will have to place your computer close to the monitor. You can purchase an extension to make your monitor cord longer, but these do not work with all monitors. If you can, try to use the cables that come with your computer without making any changes.

Ergonomics

You will also need to know a little bit about *ergonomics* to set up a comfortable workstation for your computer. *Ergonomics* is the science of designing equipment and work areas in order to maximize productivity by reducing operator fatigue and discomfort.

By using correct ergonomic devices and practices, we try to avoid the many computer-related complaints that are rampant today. These complaints are known as repetitive stress injuries (RSIs) or cumulative trauma disorders (CTDs). A recent CTDNews survey showed that 4.4 million Americans now suffer from computer-related trauma disorders.

Prevention is the key. If you set up your computer properly, you can lessen the risk of these injuries.

When you set up your work station, consider the monitor first. The monitor should be 24"-36" away from your body, if at all possible. Because of the possibility of electromagnetic radiation, you don't want to be too close to the screen. Also, it's not good for your eyes. When you set up your work area, you will realize that 36" is more than most desks will easily allow. Just do your best to stay as far from the screen as possible.

Eyestrain is a common complaint when using the computer for long periods. Glare from a light reflecting on the computer screen increases your chance of eyestrain. Try to locate your monitor where the sun and other light sources are to the side of the monitor rather then directly behind it. Overhead lighting can sometimes cause a glare. If you cannot avoid glare, you can purchase a glare guard to shield your screen. Eliminating the source of the glare is the preferable solution to this problem.

The top edge of your monitor should be at or slightly below eye level. You may need to bring the monitor up to the proper level by placing it on a small shelf or stand. This is important because putting the monitor at the proper height can lessen neck and eye strain.

The keyboard should be positioned so that your wrists are never higher than your elbows. Ideally, your elbows should be bent at a 90-degree angle and your wrists should be straight. They should not be flexed upward or bent downward. The average desk is too high to provide a good typing height. In the past, office secretaries who typed all day had a special typing table or typing extension, which was lower than the desk. When we started using computers most people put them on their desks and started typing even though the keyboard was too high for their wrists to be positioned properly for typing. This situation alone has caused much of the carpal tunnel syndrome and other computer-related wrist stress injuries. To solve this problem you may want to get a typing desk, lower your desk in some manner, raise your chair or get a keyboard drawer that allows the keyboard to sit lower than the desktop.

Next, make sure that you have a comfortable chair. Your feet should be comfortable, touching either the floor or a foot-rest. Try to get a chair with a comfortable support for your back, suitable for your body size. An adjustable chair is usually ideal.

Right now you are probably asking yourself if this is really necessary. If you plan on using the computer regularly, this will make a big difference. In today's world, we need to avoid stress as much as possible. So be discriminating in setting up your computer workstation.

Unpack and Go

Now that you have decided where to put your computer, it's time to unpack it. Be sure to remove all packing materials. This is especially important if you are unpacking a printer. There may be tape or other packing materials inside the printer.

As you unpack the computer, you will find documentation on how to set it up. There is often a card that says *Read Me First*. Don't throw this card aside. Take the time to read it! As a matter of fact, take the time to read all of the installation recommendations from the manufacturer. Many companies include an easy-to-follow instruction sheet with pictures showing how to attach each piece of hardware. For a problem-free set up, follow these instructions. Most major computer peripherals have different types of plugs. (For instance, a keyboard has a different plug than a printer, etc.) You usually don't have to worry about making a mistake if you read the instructions.

Speakers and microphones often have the same type of plug. The computer itself will be marked to show you where to plug in each of these. If you get it backwards, don't worry; the speakers won't work, but you won't blow anything up.

You might also be confused about where to plug in the telephone line. Again, the back of the computer or the modem is usually marked in some way. There will be two choices. One telephone plug is used to plug in a telephone handset, the other is used to plug in the telephone line that comes from the wall. Remember you must plug in the telephone line for your modem to work properly.

Turning the Computer On

Starting the computer is also called *booting* or *booting up* the computer. This comes from the term, "pulling yourself up by the bootstraps." When you boot the computer you will hear whirring, clicking and grinding noises. You will also see lines of text scroll quickly across your computer screen. This is a normal process that the computer goes through.

When a computer starts up it does a self-test of all of its components. It may list the item being tested and the results on the screen. This usually scrolls by too quickly to read, but it helps to diagnose a problem if anything does not pass the test.

When the computer is satisfied that everything is working properly, it looks for the operating system. An IBM-compatible computer first looks on floppy drive A. If it finds no disk in the A drive it looks on drive C, which is the hard disk. It usually finds the operating system there. It loads the operating system, and you're ready to go.

> **TIP**
>
> Do not turn anything on until you have everything set up properly.

Startup Disk

One of the first things you should do when you get your new computer is to make a startup disk. This disk is used when your computer has gotten messed up for some reason and won't start properly. If you insert this disk into your floppy drive, the computer will read the information on the disk and boot, or start from the floppy rather than from your hard disk. Once you are able to start the computer again by using this startup disk, you can then run *diagnostic software*. Diagnostic software can detect, describe and isolate a malfunction or error, enabling you to fix any problems. With any computer system, problems do arise. When they do, you will be glad that you have a startup disk.

By the way, this is also good advice for those who have never made a startup disk. You can make a startup disk at anytime. All you need is a good floppy disk.

To make a startup disk, just access *help* from your operating system, type in the words *startup disk* and follow the instructions. The whole procedure will take less than five minutes.

> *TIP* Because the computer looks at the floppy drive first, if you leave a disk in the floppy drive and reboot the computer, you will get an error. The computer will usually say something like this: "Non-system disk error, replace and press any key." Just remove the floppy, press a key and the booting process will continue properly. (This does not apply to Macs).

Register Your Hardware and Software

When you purchase new hardware or software, register your equipment or programs. Many people think that this is a waste of time; actually, it is good insurance. If a fire, flood, etc. destroys your home or office, your insurance company will probably cover the cost of your computer, but you usually do not get full value for the software that you own. If you have registered the software, you can call or write each company and they will send you another copy of the software. I have also been able to replace software that was lost or stolen in this way.

Many programs give you the opportunity to register by modem the first time you use the program. This is a great feature, and it is the easiest way to register. If you don't register by modem, you will have to mail in the registration card. Many people object to registration cards which ask you to include your life history, income level and leisure activities. To register the product, you are only required to give your name and address—you do not have to fill out any other information. Also, if you hate junk mail, attach a request that your name not be used for any mailing lists.

A Summary . . .

1. *Deciding where to put your computer is very important.*

2. *Read the installation instructions before you begin.*

3. *Understanding and applying ergonomics will protect your health and productivity.*

4. *Always make a start-up disk.*

5. *Register your hardware and software.*

How to Get the Computer To Do What You Want

Chapter 5

"The art of life is the art of avoiding pain; and he is the best pilot, who steers clearest of the rocks and shoals with which it is beset."

— *Thomas Jefferson*

It is certainly true that life has many rocks and shoals that we must avoid. The same holds true in the computer world. The number one rule here is . . . **be confident!** Realize that you are in charge of the computer. You are the one giving the orders.

There is no reason for alarm or anxiety. Millions of people have learned to drive cars and millions have already mastered the computer. You can, too.

You may be thinking that your anxiety is justified. What if you *crash* the hard drive or the machine goes up in smoke? The chances of you doing something to *crash* the hard drive are actually quite small. A hard drive *crash* is when your data storage unit (hard drive) locks itself up and refuses to cooperate. Most hard drive *crashes* are caused by hardware failure, and they are not as common as the average person thinks they are.

So, relax and realize that the computer will help you make your life easier, if you only let it.

"Nothing in life is to be feared. It is only to be understood."

— *Marie Curie*

Undo, Escape, Get Out of Trouble

The biggest fear people have in using computers is their fear of making a mistake. Mr. Rogers and Big Bird and many others from the children's world have songs and sayings that teach children that it's okay to make mistakes because everyone makes a mistake at one time or another. This is also a good lesson for adults.

Computer software manufacturers are aware that everyone makes mistakes. That's why most programs today have a miraculous option called the *Undo* button. This is really

not a button at all. It is usually a little icon on the toolbar, which is at the top or bottom of the computer screen when you are working in a program. (An icon is a small picture on your computer screen.) The icon generally has a backward arrow on it something like this: ↵. As you begin to learn a software program, the *Undo* button is a good place to start. Depending on the program, the button might be called something else, but it is usually available in some form. This button *undoes* your last command. So, if you just typed something and then hit the *Undo* button, the typing will disappear. If you just changed the size or location of some text, hitting the Undo button will return the text to its previous size and/or location.

Every program works slightly differently. Some programs will only undo your last command, some will undo up to ten previous commands. Many programs even have a *Redo* button so that if you change your mind, you can redo what you have just undone. In most cases, you have to hit the *Undo* button as soon as you realize that something has gone wrong, and before you do anything else. If you don't do this immediately, you can still correct your error. We'll discuss how further on.

There are basically three times when you can use the *Undo* button with great success. First when you have done something that is incorrect: *Undo* will eliminate your mistake and allow you to do it again correctly. Second, use the *Undo* key when you have done something that does not produce the results that you expected. Hitting the *Undo* button allows you to try again, to accomplish your task in a different way. Third, use it when you do not know what you did. Say you are working on the computer and suddenly your screen looks like garbage, or you have been transported to a different area in your letter or your spreadsheet. When this happens, you have usually hit an unusual keystroke by mistake. Someone leaning over the keyboard or dropping something on it will cause some very unusual results. If that ever occurs, don't waste time trying to figure out what happened. Just hit *Undo*. It can be a real life-saver.

The computer also has a key on the keyboard that is useful in tense situations. It is the key marked ESC, which stands for *escape*. It is called the escape key for a very good reason: It will often allow you to escape to the previous screen. If you get in a situation where you don't know what to do—try hitting the escape key.

"Any man may make a mistake; none but a fool will persist in it."

— *Marcus Tullius Cicero*

Try and Try Again

Sometimes the computer doesn't respond the way you want it to. You press a certain sequence of keys and expect a certain response. What do you do? The human tendency is to keep on trying. People often try the same thing over and over and over again. Most of the time this is fruitless. Try something once. If it doesn't work, try it again because you might have accidentally hit an incorrect key. Then you try it a third time, just to be sure. However, if the computer still doesn't respond properly, it's time to evaluate the situation. Look at the situation from the computer's angle. Think about these things:

What kind of input is the computer looking for here?

Am I using the proper key?

Is there a different approach that I could be using?

The Answer Might Be Right Before Your Eyes

To answer these questions, read everything on the screen very carefully. There is often information on the bottom line of the screen that tells you what the computer is doing. You may notice something that can give you some idea of what you need to do.

This can't be stressed too much since most people really don't look at the details the computer is showing them. Sometimes, you need to get up and step away from the computer. Have some coffee, or get a breath of fresh air. When you return, your new outlook may help you find the solution. Remember, finding the solution to a computer problem often takes a little detective work. Don't become frustrated if you don't find the solution immediately.

Once I had a call about an important spreadsheet where all the numbers had mysteriously vanished. I could see from the top of the screen that the numerical information was in place, but I couldn't see it on the screen, and it wouldn't print. Well, that problem took a little sleuthing. I asked myself why we couldn't see the numbers if the computer knew that they were there. We checked the screen, then we looked at the way the spreadsheet was designed. That's where we found the answer. The spreadsheet user had inadvertently changed one of the settings, changing the color of the print to white. So there was white print on a white background. To our eyes, the print was invisible. A click of the button to change the print back to black solved the problem.

So, remain calm and scrutinize the situation carefully. You will often find an easy solution. Remember to look for the simple answers first.

Looking for the Reason Why

After you have solved the problem, it is not necessary to figure out what went wrong, unless the problem is a recurring one. When computers are running several different applications and something goes wrong, it may be impossible to find out what caused the problem. Often the problem can be something completely unseen and untraceable, like a power surge or brownout. So, if you rebooted the computer, or in some way solved the problem with no other adverse effects, don't worry about it!

Help Screens and Manuals

This seems like a good place to talk about computer *help* screens and computer manuals. Just a few years ago technically oriented people were the only ones who used computers. The manuals were written using complex technical terms. Although we have come a long way since then, computer manuals and even *help* screens are not yet as easy to use as we would like them to be. Part of the problem is that often the computer user doesn't know what word to use as his reference. It is like trying to find the local garbage company in the yellow pages. Do you look under garbage or trash, or should you try refuse?

One of the best ways to understand many of the computer terms is to become familiar with them by reading *help* screens and/or manuals. If this is extremely boring, you will find that many of the newer programs have *help wizards* that appear to help you when you try to do something new. Some programs also have tips that appear everyday to give you suggestions on how to use the program. Don't turn these wizards or tips off until you are familiar with the program, and be sure to read them when they appear. They will help you learn the terms more quickly. For example, if you are working in a word processing program, you will need to understand terms such as *font*, *tab*, *indent* and *typeface*. If you are working in a drawing program you will have to understand terms such as *group*, *combine*, *marquee* and *skew*. The tips and wizards will help you.

Computer Rejection

Do you ever feel like the computer has rejected you? Probably most of us have had that feeling. It's the feeling you get when the computer screen freezes or when the command that you have comfortably used every day does not seem to work properly. There is an old standby routine that often works in such situations.

Exit from your program if you can. Exit Windows if you are in Windows, and then turn the computer off. Wait a minute or two and turn the computer back on. Be patient and wait for a minute or two. You need to allow the fan and hard drive and other moving parts to stop completely before you start them again. If you turn the machine on and off too quickly you will cause unnecessary strain on the moving parts. If your computer has a reset button you can simply press that instead of turning the computer on and off. (In computer terms starting or restarting the computer is called *booting or rebooting* the computer.)

This will often solve the problem. The computer can have any number of internal conflicts: There can be two programs running that conflict with each other; even the order in which the programs are running can cause a problem. Resetting the computer by turning it off and on again allows the computer to catch its breath and start over again. We all need to do that now and then.

"Make it a point to do something every day that you don't want to do. This is the golden rule for acquiring the habit of doing your duty without pain."

— Mark Twain

How to Avoid Frustration

Mark Twain's statement applies to your entire life, but it also applies to the computer in terms of what we call house-keeping chores.

The biggest complaint when it comes to computers has to do with a single word—*frustration*. People often become frustrated because of their lack of preparation. There are certain things that need to be done to make your work with the computer more productive. Many of these are simple things that most people ignore because they don't want to take the time.

Do you know where your computer manuals are? Do you know the telephone number of your computer manufacturer? These are simple housekeeping chores that will make using your computer easier. Somewhere down the road you will be glad that you did them.

Make a list of the pertinent data on your computer such as serial numbers, amount of memory, size of hard disk, etc. The best time to do this, of course, is right after you purchase the computer. However, if you have a computer and have not done this yet, you can usually find this information on your invoices, in the manuals or by calling your computer manufacturer and giving him the serial number of your machine. Then, make another list with the telephone numbers of the manufacturers of your products. Since the hours of computer manufacturers vary dramatically, it is also useful to write down the hours that they are open. Do this for all of your hardware including printers, modems, scanners and other *peripherals*.

Then add all the software that you own to the list. Telephone numbers, version numbers and serial numbers are important here. Software is updated regularly. When an update occurs, the manufacturer will update the version number, so it is important to know what version of the software you are using. Every time that you buy a new piece of hardware or software, you need to update your lists. To make it easier, I have included a computer diary in the back of this book for your use.

A Place for Everything and Everything In Its Place

The next step is to gather all your computer manuals into one place. When you look into your computer software and hardware boxes you will find a lot of paper. First, pull out all the miscellaneous flyers and promotions and keep or throw them away according to your whim. Next, add the name of the item and the manufacturer's name to your list. Then file your invoice, and pull out the manuals. A product can have as many as five manuals or, if on CD-ROM, may not have a manual at all. If they do have manuals, you need to have access to them. Put them all in one place. If your program came on floppy disks, you obviously need to save them as well. If you have the space you can keep the manuals and disks in the boxes they came in. However, all those boxes can be bulky. Many people buy a file box for the disks and keep the manuals on a bookshelf.

Whatever your filing system, you need to know where your manuals, disks, and CD-ROMS are. Even though this is an easy task, it is the easy tasks that are often the ones left undone. In my consulting business, I find that most people cannot find their manuals. I have been in offices and watched while employees searched desk after desk and room after room. The same thing happens in homes. Know where your manuals are.

Everyday Chores

There are other housekeeping chores that are necessary to avoid frustration. These chores have to do with everyday activities. Keep you programs up-to-date. Take a little extra time to do the things that will make your life easier in the future.

For example, if the type in your word processing program is set to 10 points, you probably change the type to a larger font size, such as 12 points, every time you start a letter. What a waste of time! You can easily change the settings so that they stay changed! The settings that each program uses at startup are called *default* settings. Changing the startup (default) settings on frequently used software can be a great timesaver. Click on the *help* button and put in the word *default*. If you prefer, look it up in the manual. Either way, you can customize the standard choices for your software.

Most people think they can use their instincts to put something together, rather than reading and following the

written instructions. Many of us have spent a frustrating Christmas Eve trying to put together a toy without reading the directions. Once you become familiar with your computer, you will be able to do many things instinctively, without looking in the manual or at the help screens. In the meantime, however, you need to take the extra time to look things up on a daily basis. Learn some of the things the computer can do for you.

We are lucky to be working on operating systems such as Macintosh or Windows. In older DOS or Unix programs you had to learn the ins and outs of each program separately. With Windows or Macintosh, you will find that most programs do things in the same or a similar way. This cuts down on the time it takes to learn new software. But it does not eliminate it completely. Devote a little extra time on the computer each day to learning new things and making your programs work the way you want them to. This will be time well spent.

Working With Files

Every application uses files in much the same way. You will usually see a menu on the top of your computer screen. *File* will be the first choice. When you click on the word File, a drop-down menu will appear.

After you learn your way around this File menu, you will be able to handle files in almost any program. Here are a few of the frequently-used items from a typical File menu.

New opens a new file. This will give you a blank word processing document, a blank spreadsheet or an empty database, depending on your program.

Open will open an existing file. This gives you the opportunity to work on or edit a file that you have previously created. A list will appear of all existing files. When you choose the appropriate file, the computer will load it into memory and you will see it on your screen.

Save copies the file that you have just created or edited from the computer memory to the hard disk or floppy disk for more permanent storage. When you save a new file, you are prompted for a file name and asked to choose a place to put the file. You can save the file on your hard disk or on a floppy and you can choose to put your file in the folder of your choice.

Save As lets you make a copy of your file with a different name. This is useful when you want to call up a document, make a few changes and save both the new document and the old one.

Page Setup allows you to choose margins and other pertinent information to determine how your page looks.

Print allows you to send the document to the printer. You can also print only a portion of the document or print more than one copy. If you have more than one printer, you can choose the printer that you want to use from this menu.

Print Preview will show you what your document will

When you see a letter underlined in a menu choice, it means that there is a keyboard shortcut for that item. Holding down the key marked "Alt" and pressing the underlined letter at the same time will produce the same results as clicking the mouse on the word. For example:

F̲ile = Alt + f

Fo̲rmat = Alt +o

look like when you print it out. Using print preview will save you time and printing supplies.

Close will close the file that you are working on without closing the entire program.

Exit or Quit will close your files as well as the application. You should save your files before you close the program, but most programs will help you by asking you if you want to save when you exit.

The Edit Menu

Although some programs may vary, most have the following items on their *Edit Menu*.

Undo will undo your last action.

Redo will redo what you have just undone.

Cut will delete the chosen section. Drag your mouse across the words, phrases or numbers that you wish to cut. This highlights them. Then choose Edit. Then choose Cut. The highlighted parts are deleted.

Copy will make a copy of the chosen section and store it in the *clipboard* (which is a part of the computer's memory), without changing the highlighted text.

Paste will put the chosen section wherever you have the cursor placed. The selection remains in the clipboard until you replace it with another selection or close the program.

You will find these five items to be some of the most powerful computer commands. Undo and redo will get you out of trouble quite often. Cut, copy and paste commands work between programs as well as within a program. That means that you can cut or copy data from your spreadsheet and paste it into your word processing program, and vice versa. This minimizes retyping; it saves time and increases accuracy.

Keyboard Shortcuts

The computer mouse was a wonderful invention, but there are times then it is inconvenient to use. When you are typing a document, it is often easier to use a *keyboard shortcut* instead of taking your hand off the keyboard to use the mouse. In most programs, you will see the shortcut listed after the item on a menu. For example, if you click on the word File on the menu bar, the drop down menu will give you a list of options. To the right of these options the shortcut is listed. The shortcut will give you two keys to press, usually the Control or Alt key and one other alphabetical or numerical key. You press both keys at the same time to invoke the command. It is usually easier to put your

finger on the first key, hold it down, and then press the second key. Here are some common shortcuts that will work in most programs.

Save	Ctrl+S
Cut	Ctrl+X
Copy	Ctrl+C
Paste	Ctrl+V
Print	Ctrl+P

Organize Your Files

Another way to avoid frustration is to keep your computer files in order. Again the Macintosh and Window's operating systems make this much easier than older systems. To delete old files, you simply press the delete key or drag the file to the wastebasket on your computer desktop. Working with files is the one place where Windows 95 is superior.

In older systems, including previous Windows versions, file names were an obstacle. You were limited to using eight characters, a period, then three more characters for file names. Spaces could not be used. File names were often something nonsensical like "sumtxinf.doc." Windows 95 has eliminated the length restriction and thereby will allow you to call the same file something much more descriptive, such as "Summary of Tax Information."

For many, this alone is enough reason to start using Windows 95. You will have more control over your files if their names can tell you their content. Even with Windows 95, however, you still need to take the time to delete old files, and make sure that your files are in the correct place.

When deciding how best to store your documents, imagine a filing cabinet with master folders and sub-folders. Your hard disk is the filing cabinet. The metaphor of a file drawer is appropriate. If your computer file cabinet is stuffed with files without an orderly pattern, you will have a hard time finding things, and this disorderly state can also cause computer problems. Begin with a good filing system by creating folders for the files that you use. Every time you write a letter, or create a spreadsheet or presentation, you are creating a file. The computer will usually put that file in a default directory or folder. Create document folders for the various types of work that you do, such as home, office, taxes, financial, etc. Or you might want to separate your folders by users, naming them John, Susie, Jim, etc. Find a scheme that will work for you. The important point is to have a plan and to follow it. Creating folders for your files is an easy way to keep your computer organized.

> *"Anything that can possibly go wrong, will go wrong."*
>
> — *Murphy's Law*

Computers and Murphy's Law

Most of you have probably heard of Murphy's Law, and most of you have seen it in action in your lives. Murphy's Law, it seems, is always in effect in the computer world. Whenever something can go wrong, it will, usually when we are rushed and hurried. The way to avoid this problem, in general, is not to be rushed and hurried. This is obviously an idealistic concept that cannot always be carried out, but try. If you need to do your taxes on the computer, don't start on April 14th. Give yourself some extra time. If you can possibly type your business proposal a day before it is due, do so. Time constraints always lead to frustration, and in the computer world frustration is what we need to avoid.

Make Use of Your Computer

It is often said that many humans use only about 10% of their brain's capacity. The same could be said of computers in this way: Many humans only make use of about 10% of their computer's capacity.

Don't let this happen to you. A computer represents a sizable investment. When making a computer purchase, be sure that you allocate some money for software. Especially important, make sure you set aside the time you will need to learn how to make your computer do what you want it to do.

If you run a small business, don't expect your employees to educate themselves. Institute an educational program for them. Include this education as an up-front cost so you will be sure to follow through.

Your computer can only improve your life if you let it. Invest the time and the money . . . reap the benefits for a life-time.

A Summary . . .

1. Rule number one: be confident.

2. Get out of trouble with undo or escape.

3. Avoid frustration by organizing your computer equipment and manuals.

4. Always allow yourself enough time to produce the quality of work you expect from your computer.

Portable Computing

◆

Chapter 6

"Even when I was young I suspected that much might be done in a better way."

— *Henry Ford, Sr.*

Computers continue to shrink in size. They have gotten so small that some of them are no bigger than a notebook. For the millions of users who own portable computers, this is a definite advantage.

Portable computers can do everything that your desktop computer can. The new portables have built-in CD-ROMs, Pentium chips and many other features. Portables have only two drawbacks: Their screen size is smaller and their keyboards are not full size. However, if you need to use a computer on the road, these machines are dynamite. Some people consider buying a portable for home use because of their small size.

Docking Stations

Most portable computers have ports for adding a full-size monitor and a full-size keyboard. Others have what is called a *docking station*, a small box that the portable fits into which allows you to add a full-size monitor and other peripherals. In effect, it will turn your portable computer into a desktop computer. If you are thinking of buying a portable, but will be using it at home or the office more than on the road, consider these options.

Notebook vs Laptop

There are basically three types of portable computers: The *notebook, sub-notebook* and the *laptop*. The notebook computer is smaller, the size of a notebook or tablet. The sub-notebook is even smaller. These computers usually achieve their smaller size by making the floppy disk drive separate from the computer. You still get a $3^1/2"$ drive, but instead of it being built into the computer, it comes as a small square unit that you plug into the notebook when you need it. The keyboards on notebooks usually double up on the keys to achieve their smaller size. To access certain keys, you will have to press another key at the same time, somewhat like using the shift key on a typewriter. Although this doesn't sound daunting, in everyday use it is aggravating.

Laptop computers are slightly larger because they have a built-in floppy drive. They take their name from the fact that they fit comfortably into your lap. These machines are generally superior to the notebook, if you don't mind their added size and weight.

The difference between these three types of machines is blurring. Some manufacturers call all their portable computers notebooks. To make sure that you are purchasing the correct computer, check the statistics on the size, weight and integrated equipment.

Batteries

If you expect to use your portable for computing away from your desk, you should be concerned about the type of battery your computer will use. When you purchase a portable, note the length of time that the manufacturer says the battery charge will last. I would also advise you to read reviews of the machine you are interested in buying in some computer magazines. These reviews will compare the time the manufacturer says the battery will last with the time that it lasts in actual use. These two times are often quite different. The best battery seems to be the lithium-ion battery as it provides about twice as much power as the nickel-metal-hydride batteries.

TIP

Purchase an extra battery pack if you travel extensively. Be sure to have it fully charged the day before your big presentation.

Batteries for portables need to be charged before use. Completely discharging the battery before you recharge it will extend the battery's life. However, even if you take the best possible care of your battery, it will eventually wear out. A battery can only be recharged a certain number of times before it will expire. It is not unusual to purchase a new battery every year.

Input Devices

Portable computers do not use a conventional mouse. One of several input devices are used to replace it. The *track ball* is a movable ball that is attached to one of the outside edges of the keyboard. You move your finger over the ball to position the cursor on the screen. Then you hit a nearby key to simulate the click of the mouse.

Another option is the *integrated pointing device*, which is sometimes called a *pointing stick*. This is a small stick that is located in the middle of the keyboard. You use your finger to push the stick in the direction you want the cursor to move. The stick is pressure sensitive, so the harder you push, the faster the cursor will move. Again, there will be a nearby key to press instead of clicking the mouse. The advantage of the integrated pointing device is that you do not have to take your hands off the keyboard to use it.

The *touchpad* is another input device that can be used instead of a mouse. It is a small area near the keyboard, which is flat and has a touch-sensitive surface. You control the movement of the cursor by moving you finger across the touchpad. You click on the touchpad once or twice to simulate clicking the mouse.

The choice of input devices is a matter of personal preference. Make sure, however, that the device and the key to press are located in a useful place on the computer. Some input devices are cumbersome to use. I have even seen track balls that are virtually impossible for a left-handed person to use, because of their location. Try out the input device before you buy.

PCMCIA

When you buy a portable computer it will probably come with PCMCIA slots. PCMCIA stands for Personal Computer Memory Card International Association. These are the equivalent to the expansion slots in a desktop machine. The most popular PCMCIA card is a modem. The PCMCIA card looks like a credit card, and it slides right into the computer. In two seconds you have just added a modem to your computer. These cards can also be used to add memory, network adapters and hard drives to a portable computer. There are two different sizes of PCMCIA cards. Most computers can accommodate both sizes. Investigate which PCMCIA cards you are interested in so you can be sure your computer will accommodate them.

Don't Let That Portable Weigh You Down

Another consideration in buying a portable is weight. The size and weight vary considerably from manufacturer to manufacturer. If you want a CD-ROM or other extras, they will add to the weight of the machine. Like most people, you will probably become attached to your portable computer and will wind up carrying it wherever you go. A pound or two can make a big difference. Consider how much you will use it and how strong you are when you evaluate the machine. Be aware of one other thing. When you travel, you will not only carry the computer, you will carry other things, like a spare battery, the power cord, floppy disks, etc. Find out the size the battery and how much it weighs. Find out what type of power cord the machine uses. The older cords have a power block in the middle of the cord. These blocks can be quite inconvenient and heavy to carry around. The newer machines have the power supply built into the machine and come with a normal cord. This is the preferred way to go.

The last consideration in buying a portable computer will be the price. You will pay a premium for portability.

The Screen

Since the screen on a portable is much smaller than the monitor on a desktop computer, it is important to make sure that the display is adequate for your needs.

Most portables use a *Liquid Crystal Display* (LCD). This type of display consists of energized, rod-shaped crystals that move and bend light. The direction of the crystals creates the picture. That is why on some portable machines, you must look at the screen from the proper angle to see it clearly.

One type of LCD is the passive-matrix. The picture is sharp and clear as long as you view it from the proper angle. This display tends to refresh, or redraw more slowly because it changes the image by modifying the crystals all at once. Because of this slow refresh rate, many manufacturers offer a dual-scan passive-matrix display. Dual-scan splits the screen in two. This doubles the lines that can be changed at one time and speeds up the display considerably.

An active-matrix display is the closest in quality to the display that you usually find on desktop computers. It is called active because its own transistor produces each individual *pixel*, or picture element. This results in a much sharper and clearer image. It is also better when viewed from an angle. Since this technology requires additional hardware, active-matrix screens are always more expensive than passive-matrix displays.

Infrared Ports

Many portable computers are equipped with infrared ports. Since many printers also have these ports built in, you can send information from your portable to your printer in a wireless fashion. This technology is similar to what is used on the remote control of your television. This is a useful feature for road warriors who do all their work off-site and only come into their home or office to print up their documents.

Care and Feeding of Your Portable

The care of portable computers is relatively straight-forward. However, many porta-bles have been fried, melted or destroyed by well-meaning people who didn't think about what they were doing. Here are some pitfalls to avoid:

- Avoid dropping, bumping or jarring the computer as much as possible.

- Keep liquids away from your computer.

- Keep your computer away from electromagnetic fields. Don't place it down next to any large pieces of mechanical equipment.

- Don't set the portable down in front of an air conditioner or on top of a radiator.

- Always use a surge protector for your portable. You can buy small surge protectors especially designed for portable computers.

- Avoid rapid changes in temperature and/or humidity. If possible, let the computer adjust to the temperature of the room before using it.

- Don't move the portable when it is on, especially if the hard drive is working.

Traveling With Your Portable

- Backup your hard disk before you take a trip.

- Carry a spare emergency *boot disk* with you. A boot disk contains the operating system for your computer.

- Only plug your portable into outlets that are correctly wired and of the proper voltage. You will need an adapter for many foreign countries.

- Your modem may also need an adapter for foreign telephone lines. Check this out before you leave.

- Label all your equipment with name, address and telephone number. Cables and power supplies are often left behind in hotel rooms.

- Carry a copy of proof of purchase in case it's needed for a custom's check.

- Carry a list of technical support telephone numbers for all your hardware and software companies. Also be sure that you have applicable registration or serial numbers with you.

- Don't worry about airport X-ray machines in the United States and Europe. They will not harm your data.

- Keep your computer in your sight at all times. Theft of portable computers is a common occurrence.

Personal Digital Assistants

These small hand-held computers haven't yet reached their full potential. They are good for communications, reading E-mail and keeping your address book handy. Most have either an awkward keyboard or a pad which you write on with a plastic stylus. Once they find a way to input information more easily, they will become powerful little machines.

A Summary . . .

1. *Portable computers vary in size and weight.*

2. *You can use a docking station to make your portable more like a desktop computer when not on the road.*

3. *Important features include input devices, type and size of screen and type of battery.*

4. *Portable computers have special care instructions.*

5. *Be prepared before you travel with your portable.*

Protecting Your Investment

———◆———

Chapter 7

"You're never wrong to do the right thing."

— *Malcolm Forbes*

When you purchase a car, there are certain things you do to protect it from unnecessary damage. You change the oil regularly, keep it clean, rotate the tires and occasionally tune it up. The same is true for your computer. Although computer prices have consistently fallen, a new computer still represents a sizable investment worth protecting.

Surge Protectors

The best way to protect your computer is to purchase a good *surge protector*. Without a surge protector, a power surge that occurs because of lightning or a power spike, can travel down the electric or telephone line with the force equivalent to a tidal wave. It can completely zap your computer equipment.

Other less dramatic power problems, such as blackouts or brownouts, can and do occur on a regular basis, sometimes without our awareness of them. A recent study by IBM showed that a typical computer is subject to more than 120 power problems per month. That means the average computer encounters about four power anomalies in a single day. The effect of these power problems can range from subtle things like keyboard lockups to severe problems like a burnt-out modem or motherboard.

A surge protector is simply a device that looks something like a strip of outlets. You plug your computer equipment and your telephone line (if your computer has a modem) into the surge protector and plug the surge protector into the wall. Then, if a power surge occurs, the surge protector will intercept it before it is able to reach your computer.

Lightning Strikes Often

A company that specializes in power protection components uses a bolt of lightning in its ads. Under the lightning, the words read "It's not if . . . it's when." This ad is true for people living in areas of our country where lightning storms are a common occurrence. No matter where you live, however, lightning is a fact of life. Lightning and power surges can damage electrical equipment and can even destroy such equipment. Even a slight jolt of lightning can cause hardware degradation and data loss.

Choosing the Right Protection

A good surge protector is inexpensive compared to the cost of replacing your computer equipment. It is one of the wisest computer investments that you can make.

When it comes to power protection equipment, you usually get what you pay for. Cheap surge protectors offer very little protection. Don't confuse a surge protector with a power strip. A power strip basically enables you to plug many items into one outlet. Power strips look similar to surge protectors, but are less expensive and offer no protection at all. Don't skimp; spend a little more if you have to, and get a good surge protector.

TIP

Buy a surge protector that will accommodate all of your equipment. Because of slight differences in electrical currents, it is best to plug all equipment into the same source.

There are basically two things to look for in a surge protector. First, make sure that the unit covers lightning strikes. Some surge protectors only cover power surges and spikes and do not give any coverage for lightning. Second, look for a unit that offers to repair or replace connected equipment that is damaged by all surges including lightning. This type of replacement coverage varies in its amount. A good surge protector will usually offer $10,000 to $25,000 worth of coverage. That means the manufacturer of the surge protector will reimburse you up to that dollar amount for any equipment damaged by a power surge while properly plugged into their unit. Be sure to send in your warranty card, which is required by most companies before the coverage takes effect.

If you have a modem on your computer, buy a surge protector that also offers protection for the telephone line. You will find a place on the unit to plug in your telephone cord. It is common for a computer to be hit with a power surge that travels through the telephone lines. If your modem telephone line is not plugged into the surge protector your equipment is susceptible to damage.

Backup Power Supply

While considering surge protection, you might also want to investigate UPS protection. *UPS*, in this case, stands for "uninterrupted power supply." UPS units give you surge protection plus battery backup power. Power glitches are common. You have probably encountered them. When the power goes off, even if only for a second, sometimes your computer goes off completely. You lose your work and risk damaging open files. A UPS will keep your computer working when the power flickers on and off. If the power goes off completely, the UPS will allow you to keep working for a certain period of time, enabling you to save your files properly and shut your computer off without any damage or loss of data. You will pay a premium for this kind of protection. However, if you are using a computer for your office or are working with important data, you definitely want to look at one of these units.

Providing the Right Environment

The first computers that I worked with in 1968 were enormous pieces of machinery taking up a room that was bigger than the average three-bedroom apartment. At that time, large companies such as banks and insurance companies were the only ones with computers. The computer was kept in a special climate-controlled room with air conditioning and humidity set to exacting levels. The room also had special static-free floors.

The personal computers we work on today are not as fussy as the early monstrous computers. But we still fight the same three vicious enemies: heat, humidity and static electricity. I once saw the inside of a computer that had operated in 95-degree weather with about 90% humidity. When it stopped working, it was opened up to reveal a mess of corrosion, rust, and goo. So be sure to keep the air conditioner on if the weather heats up.

Watch out for static electricity, especially during the drier winter months or if you live in a dry climate. Static can act like a magnet to a computer. It has been known to scramble the information on a disk and make the computer act strangely. I was once called to a company that was having trouble with their computers. As I walked into the office in question, I could feel my clothing cling to my body from the static electricity in the air. Once they bought a small humidifier and several cans of static guard, this problem was solved.

You've made a significant investment in your computer. An easy way to protect it is to keep your computer's environment controlled. Moderation is the key word here. Don't let your computer room get too hot, too cold, too humid or too dry.

A Dust-Free Environment

Dust and smoke are two other computer enemies that were carefully controlled in the first "Computer Rooms." Unless you have a special air filter on your furnace, you probably have dust in your home. Computers of today will survive in most normal home or office environments. However, there are a few things that you can do to keep your computer as dust free as possible. First, keep the area as clean and uncluttered as possible. Keep pets away from the computer. Most dust accumulates on the floor, so keep your computer on a desk or table, if you can. Carpets attract more dust than bare floors, so if you have a choice, keep your computer in an uncarpeted room. Keep smoke and ashes away from your computer.

All that said, we now have to come down to reality. The reality is that you will probably put your computer in a carpeted room and, if you smoke, you will want to enjoy a cigarette while you work on the computer. So use good sense. Keep your ashes away from the keyboard and the computer and buy a can of compressed air. Cans of compressed air come with a little straw that you attach to the nozzle. You can use this to clean your keyboard easily. Then open the computer case and spray the dust off the components and away from the computer. You will find dust accumulates heavily around the fan power supply. In most cases, you will be able to see how much dust has accumulated just by looking at the back of the computer. Doing this once a year is enough in most situations. This type of regular cleaning will keep you from having to replace your fan or power supply when it becomes clogged with dust balls. And keep in mind that if your fan stops working because it is clogged with dust, your computer will probably overheat and cause severe damage to the components.

"If you do the little jobs well, the big ones will tend to take care of themselves."

— Dale Carnegie

Easy Everyday Maintenance

Fortunately there is little you have to do to maintain your computer. A light dusting is about all it takes. If your computer screen needs cleaning, just spray some mild window-type cleaner on a cloth and wipe the screen clean. Don't spray any liquids, such as window cleaner directly on the computer or the computer monitor. Liquids can damage computer components. Be sure to keep your drinks as far away from the computer as possible.

Although computers are solid pieces of machinery, they have connections and cards that can become loose if they are jostled, jarred or shaken. Don't move your computer any more than necessary. If you must move it to another location, try to retain the original boxes to repack.

Don't unplug cables from your computer or printer when the equipment is turned on.

Cleaning Your Mouse

If your mouse becomes difficult to move around or seems to have a mind of its own, it may be time to give your mouse a good cleaning. Turn your mouse over and rotate the little donut-shaped disk and remove the ball that is inside of the mouse. A soft dry cloth is usually adequate for cleaning the ball itself. If the ball looks dirty you can clean it with some water and dry it thoroughly. The problem is usually caused not by the ball, but by dirt in the areas that touch the ball. If you look inside the bottom of the mouse after the ball has been removed, you will see some small bars or rollers that the ball touches as it rotates. Dip a cotton swab in water or isopropyl alcohol and clean the dirt off these bars. You might have to do this as often as once a month, depending on the type of mouse you own.

It a good idea to always use a mouse pad. If your mouse needs cleaning often, you might want to replace the pad.

Leave It On or Turn It Off

Should you keep your computer on all the time, or turn it on and off as you need it? There are many die-hard, knowledgeable folks on each side of this issue. Here are the facts. Every time you turn the computer on there is a power surge that is stressful on several of the computer's components. Some say that turning the computer on and off will make those components wear out prematurely. If, however, you leave the computer on all the time, certain other components get more wear and tear.

Those who advise you to turn your computer off as much as possible are also concerned that excessive computer use needlessly adds to your electric bill, as well as the planet's usage of electricity. The Environmental Protection Agency has created a power consumption standard for computers called the Energy Star program. Most new computers and peripherals are Energy Star compliant. This means that computers are using much less electricity than they used to, so the use of electricity is not as much of a consideration.

Since no one can ultimately decide who is correct in this controversy, most intelligent people try to use some common sense in deciding whether to leave the computer on or to turn it off. I generally leave my computer on all day, unless I know that I will not be using it. This seems more logical than turning it on and off. I turn my computer off at night, which makes perfect sense to me, even though there have been nights when I get up and play on the Internet at 3 a.m.

Floppy Disk Maintenance

Older 5¼" disks were somewhat flexible and susceptible to damage. The newer 3½" floppy disks are covered by thick plastic and are much less flexible. They are extremely durable because of their hard plastic cover. The real guts of the disk are under the cover. You will notice a metal shutter on the disk.

When you insert the disk into the computer, the metal shutter is pushed to the side, allowing the computer to access the softer, more vulnerable disk surface inside.

Keep your floppy disks in the box they came in or a disk storage box. It's best to store the disk with the shutter down. This allows you to read the label more easily when the floppy disk is in the box. It also keeps the disk surface better protected.

There are two things that can easily ruin a floppy disk: heat and magnetism. It takes intense heat to destroy a floppy disk, so it is quite easy to protect them. Common sense will dictate that you don't leave a floppy disk in the sun or in a car on a hot summer day.

Protecting your disks from magnetism can be a little trickier. Magnetism can be hiding in many unsuspecting places. Every time your phone rings, it becomes magnetized. Magnets are often used to hang papers on file cabinets or refrigerators. Magnets can be found in the document holders that some typists use, as well as in containers that hold paper clips. All of these objects should be kept away from your floppy disks, as well as your hard disk.

Let me explain why magnetism can hurt disks. There is a read/write head inside your floppy drive, or your hard drive, which is used to read information from your disk and to write new information on the disk. This read/write head contains a piece of wire wrapped around a piece of iron. Electricity is run through the read/write head which magnetizes the head. The head then magnetizes minute particles of iron oxide on the surface of the disk, dividing them into two configurations, representing ones or zeros. You will remember from our discussion about how computers work that the computer uses ones and zeros to represent and interpret all data. Now that you understand that the data on disks was put there by magnetism, you can also understand why we need to keep magnets away from our computers and our floppy disks. A magnet can realign the data on a disk and cause all of the information on that disk to become scrambled. By the way, static electricity works just like a low-level magnet to scramble information on your disks.

"It is not enough to will, one has to act."

— Johann Wolfgang von Goethe

Saving Files

It is important to save a file as you create it. When you are working on a document, you need to save it on a regular basis. For instance, say you are writing a long letter to your grandmother. Since you haven't seen her for quite a while, you expect that it will take you over an hour to write the letter. As you are working on your letter, it is kept in the computer's memory. However, that computer memory is wiped out if the computer is turned off. So if you spend an hour working on your letter and you don't save it to the hard disk, it is available only in the computer memory. If, at that moment, your dog walks by and trips on the computer cord pulling the plug out of the wall, you will lose an hour's worth of work. If the power goes out for any reason or if an unruly program causes the computer to crash, whatever was in the computer's working memory is lost.

To make sure that you won't have to retype that whole letter, save your work. When you start the letter you should immediately give it a name and save it to the hard disk. Then, every ten minutes or so, hit the save icon. The program will then save the entire letter that you have written to that point by writing it to the hard disk.

> **TIP**
>
> Even if your program has an auto-save feature, you still need to save the program yourself.

Hard Drive Crashes

Once your letter has been written to the hard disk, it is fairly safe, but not completely secure. There is still the possibility that the hard drive could *crash*. When we say that the hard drive crashed, it simply means that for some reason, the hard drive is no longer able to retrieve the information that it needs to run the computer. There are many things that can cause a hard drive to crash. Magnetism or static electricity can scramble the information and make it unreadable to the computer. A hardware failure can occur that makes the hard drive unable to function properly. A vicious virus can overwrite the information that the hard drive needs to run the computer. This list can go on and on. That is why we need to backup our data, even after it has been written to the hard disk.

"Delay always breeds danger ..."

— *Miguel de Cervantes*

101

Backup Your Files

Buying a surge protector and keeping your computer clean and in the right environment will help to protect the financial investment that you made in your computer. There is another type of investment that you make. You should protect yourself against loss of time by creating a backup of your work.

Backing up files is simply the process of making an extra copy of important files. If and when something ruins a file, the backup can be used to restore that file to its original condition. When you see how easily data can be inadvertently ruined, you can understand why it is important to backup your data files.

It is good to have a backup strategy. The first thing that you must decide is what kind of medium you will use to backup your data.

The easiest way to backup data is to backup the entire hard disk. This requires a *tape drive* or a special high-capacity floppy drive often referred to as a *Zip drive* or *Jaz drive*. A Zip drive can hold 100 megabytes of data while a Jaz drive can hold one gigabyte. The tape or high-capacity floppy drive comes with its own software and backs up your entire drive at one time. Then if disaster strikes, you simply restore the files from the backup tape or disks. This is the best method if you want a quick and easy way to restore your data.

The problem is that a backup of this type can take a long time, up to several hours. Also, if you have a large hard disk you might need several tapes, or many high-capacity floppy disks. The solution to these problems is to use an *incremental backup system*. It works like this. First you do a full backup. Say you do this every week, on Monday. Then each day, you do what's called an incremental backup. This backs up only the files that have been added or have changed since the full backup. Since you are only backing up a few files, the incremental backup is accomplished quickly and easily. Now, say that your hard drive crashes on Thursday and you need to restore your data. You simply restore the files from the full backup that you did on Monday. Then you restore the files from each incremental backup that you made on Tuesday and Wednesday.

Working with tape or high-capacity floppy drives is an easy way to backup your files. If you don't have a tape or high-capacity floppy drive, you can use your floppy drive to backup your data. You could backup your entire hard disk to regular floppy disks, however few people would enjoy feeding 100 or 200 disks into the computer every time they wanted to do a full backup. So if you are using a floppy drive to backup you will want to backup only your important data files. If your hard drive crashes or some other disaster occurs, you will have to go through the trouble of reinstalling all of your programs from their original disks. But the precious data that you spent hours creating and the important names, addresses, numbers and other personal information will still be intact. There are several ways to backup your data to floppy disks. Many programs allow you to hit a backup icon and choose the floppy disk as the place to backup to. If your program doesn't have that option, you can simply save the file to the floppy. Or as often as you think necessary, copy all your important files to floppy disks. Most operating systems have their own built-in backup program.

Have a Backup Strategy

Assuming that you have now decided which type of medium you will use to backup, the next step is to decide how often you will backup your files. The best rule of thumb I can give you is this, if you have entered a considerable amount of information into your computer and you would not like to have to do all that work over again, then back it up. Consider how much work you can do in a day. If you would not want to lose the work that you accomplished in a day, then backup every day. If you don't change or add too many files each day, you might want to backup on a weekly basis. The key is to have a schedule in place. Knowing that you should backup your files every Wednesday is preferable to just knowing that you should backup your files.

Whether you use tapes or floppies for your backup, be sure to rotate them, and if possible, keep several copies. For instance, if you are only interested in backing up the files from your financial program, back them up every day and put them on a floppy disk. However, don't use the same floppy each time. You might want to use three floppy disks and rotate them, using a different one each day. Remember that floppy disks will wear out after many uses. After a few months or a year, you will need to replace the floppies that you are using with new ones.

Proper labeling is also an important part of backing up. Be sure to label your tape or disk with the date and contents. I use special diskette labels that you can write on, erase and write on again. You need a special marker and special eraser, but I find them invaluable.

Keep Your Backups Safe

The last thing to decide is where you will keep your backup disks or tapes. Besides data loss from things like a hard drive crash, you also need to protect your computer and your data from things like fires and floods. If you have important data, you might want to store a copy at a remote site. Some people put a copy in their safe deposit box, but keeping an extra copy at a friend's or relative's house might be sufficient. When you make two sets of backup data, and keep an extra set in another location, you minimize your chance of data loss.

Don't underestimate the importance of your data. I had a client who lost all the information in her family tree because she hadn't backed up the file. She didn't think that it was an important file, until she realized that she had been working on her family history for three years. It will probably take her that long to reconstruct the information.

There is one other method of backup if you don't want the bother of buying a tape drive or remembering to backup all the time. You can pay someone else to do it for you. If you have a modem on your computer, there are several companies that will backup your data for you during the night. All you have to do is install their software, choose what you want to backup and how often, and leave your computer on. Your computer will call their computer at whatever time you choose and copy your files to their computer. If you have hard drive failure, you can retrieve your files from their computer at any time. Obviously, you will want to make sure that the company you use for this kind of service is reliable. You are putting your data in their hands, so make sure that they are using secure *servers* and encrypting (coding) the data so that your data cannot be accessed by anyone else. The server is a computer, which stores files.

Backing up your data makes good sense. It's like buying an insurance policy: You hope that you will never need it, but when disaster strikes, you will be glad that you have it.

Screen Savers

Before the days of color computer monitors, we used monochrome monitors that were subject to phosphor burn-in. If you left your computer on for a long period of time with the same image displayed on the screen, the phosphors in the area of the display would wear out. This would create a sort of ghost image of that screen that would be superimposed over anything else that you tried to display. Screen savers were special programs that were developed to prevent this from happening.

A screen saver is a program that creates some sort of moving picture or pattern that constantly changes the display on your screen and prevents the burn-in from happening. The screen saver comes on automatically when it senses that you have not used the computer for a certain period of time. The user can change the amount of time that elapses before the screen saver comes on.

Today, screen savers are not needed to protect your screen or any other part of your computer, for that matter. Most color monitors today are not affected by phosphor burn-in. Instead of dying a natural death once color monitors were introduced screen-saver programs have become quite popular. Everyone enjoys watching these moving images. Program developers capitalize on this by creating some fantastic screen savers that are so colorful and so much fun that the public can't resist buying them. A screen saver won't help you protect your computer investment, but it can put some fun in your life.

Hard Disk Maintenance

The hard disk is a very important part of your computer. Since all of your important data is stored there, you want to make sure you keep it working at peak performance.

The first thing to remember is to always *exit* your programs properly. When you are finished using a program, terminate it by choosing *close* or *exit* from the menu or click on the appropriate icon to close the program. You must also exit your operating system properly. For example, if you are using Windows 3.1, close all programs and exit to DOS before you turn your computer off. If you are using Windows 95, close all programs, click on the *Start* button, choose *Shut Down* and wait until your computer screen says that it is safe to turn your computer off.

Do not turn your computer off while a program is running. If you do, the computer doesn't have time to close its files properly, and it may lose track of data. Most programs today are smart enough to recover, or at least try to recover that data when you start the program again. However, pieces of data can be left on the hard disk with incomplete addresses. This may cause problems such as cross-linked files and lost information clusters which may lead to erratic behavior in the future.

Scan Disk

Hard disk problems may be the result of things you can't control or things you may not even know about. A slight power surge, a momentary brownout, or a hardware malfunction can cause them. These unknown things happen so often that computer operating systems have created a way to repair the hard disk when it encounters these problems. This is accomplished with a handy little program called *Scan Disk*, a program that is part of your operating system. For example, it is a command in DOS. In Windows 95, you will find it under *Programs*, *Accessories*, *System Tools*. You can tell Scan Disk to automatically repair all of the errors that it finds. You should use this program on a regular basis to keep your hard disk in tip-top shape.

Defragmentation

Hard disks have another problem called *disk fragmentation*. When you save a file, the computer writes that file to the hard disk. We tend to assume that the computer writes that file on the hard disk in one location, as one complete file.

This is not necessarily true. When the hard disk is new,

the file may be written to the hard disk in one large chunk. As more files are saved, and others are deleted from the hard disk, there is less and less contiguous free space available. When the computer cannot find a space large enough to fit the whole file, it breaks it up into smaller pieces. Files that are stored in several different pieces are called *fragmented files*.

Over time, your computer will accumulate many fragmented files. When you open a fragmented file, the computer must gather the pieces of that file from many different areas of the hard disk. This, of course, causes the computer to work harder and adds to the time that it takes to open the file. You can optimize the performance of your hard disk by using a program to defragment your hard disk on a regular basis. This type of program will rearrange the data on your hard disk so that each file occupies a contiguous area. Your files are contiguous when all the elements are next to each other, with nothing in between. Additionally, all the small empty spaces on the disk are combined to form a large empty space where future files can be written in one piece. A defragmentation program comes with your operating system. You can use the *help* menu or operating system documentation to locate and run the program. Defragment your hard disk on a regular basis; once a month is usually sufficient.

Scanning and defragmenting your hard disk are clean-up duties that may soon be automatically performed by the computer. In the meantime, you have two options. You can perform these operations yourself, like remembering to change the oil in your car. Or, you can buy a program that will schedule and perform these functions for you automatically. There are several programs on the market that will do this; all of them perform other valuable functions as well. You might want to check them out!

Keeping Your Computer Healthy

Computer viruses are everywhere. With the Internet and increased communication between computers, viruses are spreading faster than ever. The only way to prevent their spread is through public awareness of safe computing.

First, let me give you some idea of what a computer virus is. A computer virus is simply a set of computer instructions, or computer code, that was written by some unscrupulous person. This code is attached to some part of the normal computer operating system or computer program. The instructions in this code tell the computer to perform some destructive task such as deleting important information or crashing the hard disk.

The most usual symptom is erratic behavior. The destruction can happen at any rate of speed and can affect almost any part of the computer. The trigger that activates the virus can be almost anything. For instance the virus can be activated the minute you start your computer. It can be inside your computer in an inactive state, waiting for a certain event to happen. You may have heard of the famous Michelangelo virus, which crashes hard disks on March 6, Michelangelo's birthday.

How does your computer get a virus? Just as a human virus is passed from person to person, a computer virus is passed from computer to computer. A virus can be attached to any file that you copy to your computer. If you download files from the Internet, or copy programs or files from friends on floppy disks, you are susceptible to viruses. Actually, anytime that you download files or put a floppy disk into your computer, you are susceptible to viruses.

If your computer starts to act a little weird, the first thing to do, is to check for viruses. You can do this with an *anti-virus program.*

The best thing to do is to prevent viruses from entering your computer. Purchase a good virus protection program to check all files for viruses before they can enter your system. Once installed, an anti-virus program can be set to work in the background. It will check all files before they enter your computer and will alert you if a virus is detected before it enters your system.

You should be careful to purchase a virus protection program that matches your operating system. If you use a Mac, buy a virus protection program made especially for Macintosh computers. If you use Windows 3.1 or Windows 95, use a program that was written specifically for your operating system. If you try to use a virus protection program that was written for Windows 3.1 on a Windows 95 machine, you can mess up your computer.

Another important consideration is that new viruses are written every day. It seems that there are many people with extra time on their hands and a slightly warped idea of how to use their intelligence. With this in mind, every good company that sells virus protect programs offers frequent updates. You should make arrangements to get these updates regularly to be sure that your computer is completely protected. Most companies have a *bulletin board system (BBS)* where you can download these updates. A *bulletin board* is an electronic message center where you can send or receive messages. You can also get the updates from the Internet or a service such as CompuServe or AOL. If you do not have a modem, you can have the company mail the updates. Be sure to check this out when you purchase the program. Some companies give you a year of free updates, others do not.

Getting Technical Support

It doesn't matter whether you know a lot about computers or you know nothing at all. Sooner or later you will have to contact a hardware or software manufacturer for technical support.

TIP The company you purchased your computer from will be an important source of support for you. The computer manufacturer will support any software that came pre-installed on your computer when you bought it.

When you need help with a problem, the first question usually is, "Who do I call?" Sometimes it is hard to differentiate between a hardware or software problem. The best thing to do is to start with some simple detective work.

For example, if you can't print from a certain program, try to print from other programs. If you cannot print at all, the problem may be that the printer is not working properly, or it is not communicating with the computer. Check the cables and the *on-line* button. Print out a *printer self-test*. (See the section of this book on printers for how to do this.) Look at your operating system under *printer troubleshooting*. Look in your printer manual under *troubleshooting*. If these options don't solve the problem, call the printer manufacturer. If you are having trouble printing in only one program, call the company that produced that program. In other words, take a good look at the problem and try to determine who can help you.

If you just installed a new software program and your

computer immediately goes bonkers, or another program doesn't work properly, call the manufacturer of the program that you just installed . . . They will know of any incompatibilities with your system or with other programs.

The premise behind technical support is an easy one. You have a problem; you call and get help. Unfortunately, it doesn't always work that easily.

First of all, each company's support options are different and seem to change on a regular basis. Even though the company may have offered 24-hour service at the time you purchased, they may have changed their hours since then. Also, many companies are now charging for support that used to be free. Many offer 30, 60 or 90 days of free support, dating from the time of your first call. So, even if you have owned the program for six months, if you have never made a call to the company, you are still entitled to free technical support. Since there is no standard in place, you will have to find out how the company operates.

> **TIP** Check out the resource guide in the back of this book to aid you in finding telephone numbers, addresses and web sites for software and hardware manufacturers.

As many of you know from experience, technical support telephone lines, can be extremely busy. Long waiting times are not unusual. Most companies are attempting to improve their support lines and their support options.

On-Line Support

If your computer is operating correctly, and you have a modem, you can get technical support through the Internet or the company's bulletin board service. This is a good option for simple *how-to* questions. The address of the company's home page and their bulletin board number will usually be found in the documentation that came with the hardware or software. If you use the Internet option, you will find information that might help you. Once on-line, you can also E-mail a support technician with your question. You will usually get a reply within twenty-four hours.

Fax for Help

Many companies have a fax-back option. This option doesn't answer your question directly, but you may receive enough information to help you with your problem. To use this type of service, call the company's fax-back number.

When prompted to do so, punch in the specified number to request a directory. Then enter your fax number. They will fax you a directory of the available documents. You choose the documents that are pertinent to your problem and order those documents. This is often a good option. Sometimes you learn things about the program that you didn't know just by reading these documents.

When using the Internet or the fax-back option, you will often see a page or document called *FAQ*. This stands for "frequently asked questions." If you have a question about the software, chances are that someone has asked that question before and you can find it in the FAQ. Often these questions provide clarification to the documentation or clues to how the software works. This can be a good place to look for information.

If these other options don't work for you, call technical support. Before you do so, make sure that you have all the information that you will need for the support technician. You should be sitting in front of the computer that you are having a problem with. Know the name of the program that you are calling about, the version number and the identification number, if applicable. If you are calling about hardware, have the make, model and serial number available. It is helpful for you to know the configuration of your computer system. If you are getting an error message, write it down and be able to explain to the technician exactly what is happening.

> **TIP**
> To find the identification number for a software program, start the program and choose *Help*. You will usually see an option labeled *About (plus the program name)*. Choosing that option will give you the serial number and other program information.

A Summary . . .

1. *Lightning, power surges and glitches can damage both your computer and your data. Protect your computer investment by purchasing a good surge protector.*

2. *A suitable room environment is important to your computer's longevity.*

3. *Don't flirt with disaster. Develop a backup strategy and follow it regularly.*

4. *Do your own troubleshooting before you call for technical support.*

Expanding the Power of Your Personal Computer

---◆---

Chapter 8

"The creative mind plays with the objects it loves"

— Carl Gustav Jung

When you go shopping for a new car and look at the sticker price on the window, you will find that the base price of the car is usually reasonable. It's the options that add up. Once you add the air conditioning, automatic transmission and leather upholstery, you have tacked on a few thousand dollars to the price. Fortunately, the price tag on a computer system usually includes everything. As noted earlier, the monitor is sometimes sold separately. However, once you calculate that as well, you know exactly how much you need to spend. Right?

In this chapter I will introduce you to some of the extras that you can purchase with your computer. Some of them, like a printer, will be a necessity. Many others will be simply for fun. Knowing what's available and how these items function can make you a more confident computer consumer, whether you purchase these extras or not.

Printers

When we speak of computers we often speak of two kinds of data: input and output. Input is what you put into the computer. This might be instructions to the computer program or it might be something like the names and addresses of your friends and relatives.

Input devices are commonly things like the keyboard or the mouse.

Output is what comes out of the computer, such as the answer to a mathematical problem or an address book that you created. The two most common output devices are the monitor and the printer. You can see the output from the computer on your screen and/or you can print it out.

The term *paperless society* was bantered about when computers were first introduced. As you may know from the amount of paper found in the average home or office today, we have not made much progress toward the 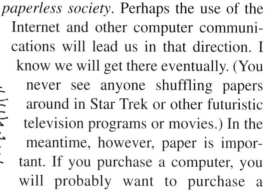 *paperless society*. Perhaps the use of the Internet and other computer communications will lead us in that direction. I know we will get there eventually. (You never see anyone shuffling papers around in Star Trek or other futuristic television programs or movies.) In the meantime, however, paper is important. If you purchase a computer, you will probably want to purchase a printer to go along with it.

There are several factors to consider when buying a printer. First, be sure that the printer you are considering will work with the computer that you have or will be buying. Most of today's printers will work with any PC. Others may only work with either an Apple product or an IBM-compatible machine, but not with both. Be sure to ask this question before you buy.

Price is usually the top consideration when you are deciding on a new purchase. Printers can range in price from a few hundred dollars to several thousands of dollars. Your price range will generally be determined by the amount of money that you have to spend, as well as the way that you plan to use the printer. Before you make any decisions, be sure to compare the cost of materials such as toner, ink cartridges and paper. This can differ dramatically from printer to printer. Also look at the size and type of paper that the printer accepts. Most printers print both letter and legal size paper. If you want to print on smaller or larger paper, make sure that the printer you choose can handle that size of paper. Also, make sure that the printer can handle envelopes, if you need that feature. There are basically three types of printers available today. They are dot-matrix, ink jet and laser printers.

Dot-Matrix Printers

Dot-matrix printers are similar to typewriters. They have small pins in the print-head that strike an inked ribbon to create a series of dots on the paper. These dots then form letters and numbers. Since this process involves the impact of the print-head against the paper, dot-matrix printers are noisy machines. This type of impact printing allows for printing on multi-part forms. Many other printers are not able to do this.

Dot-matrix printers are usually the least expensive printers, however I've seen much better output from a good typewriter than some dot-matrix printers. The printed output of a dot-matrix printer is poor compared to the output of ink jet or laser printers. Dot-matrix printers use the older type of continuous computer paper with holes on the side. Some can also accept single sheets. These printers have been generally replaced by the newer ink jet printers. However, you will continue to see dot-matrix printers, especially in office environments, because they are real workhorses.

Ink Jet Printers

Ink jet printers produce high quality documents at a relatively low cost. The ink jet printer sprays ink on the page to form the characters on a page. This produces a very clear image on the paper. Documents printed on an ink jet printer take a minute or two to dry and may be smudged if they are handled too soon, but this does not usually present a problem. Ink jets are perfect for home use and will also handle light office use. However, if you will be printing mass mailings or have any other heavy usage, you should look at purchasing a laser printer instead of an ink jet. Ink jet printers, depending on the make and model, print at different speeds. If you don't want to wait for your output, buy the fastest one you can find.

Color ink jet printers do a great job and have become quite affordable. Again, they are perfect for home use, but they are also excellent for putting a splash of color on documents that are produced for business purposes. The ink for these printers is held in small print cartridges. One cartridge usually holds the black ink and another holds the color ink.

Some printers allow you to install only one print cartridge at a time. That means if you have the black cartridge installed, and you want to print in color, you have to remove the black cartridge and install the color cartridge. In order to print something black when the color cartridge is installed, the printer combines all the colors to create black. This is a waste of color ink (which is more expensive), and it also produces a black with a slight greenish cast. This type of product will cause nothing but frustration. I find this situation unacceptable and advise you to buy a printer that allows both cartridges to be installed at the same time. You will probably pay a little more, but it will be well worth it.

Some color printers can produce photo-quality output. This requires a special color print cartridge. You can also purchase special coated paper and/or special photo-quality paper. This type of printing can get expensive because the supplies are costly, but can produce dramatic results.

When choosing an ink jet printer, whether black or color, the cost of the ink should be a concern, as it is expensive. Check this out when you compare the models. Also, different printers have print cartridges that hold different amounts of ink. It is frustrating, and can be expensive, to constantly run out of ink. If you carefully read the printer documentation or call the company, you can usually find out how many pages they expect to get from each print cartridge. Consider these numbers; they can be different for each printer.

Also remember that the color ink jet will have different speeds for printing in black and printing in color. It takes these machines longer to print a page in color. Print speeds will be listed as pages per minute (PPM).

Laser Printers

The laser printer uses a print technique that is significantly different from that of the dot-matrix or ink jet printers. In reality, it produces images in a manner similar to a photocopier. The image is drawn with a laser on a drum inside the printer. The electronic charge then attracts particles of toner in the pattern that was drawn by the laser. The drum then rolls across the paper and the electrical charge causes the toner to jump from the drum to the paper. Since the images formed by the lasers can be quite detailed, the print quality of laser printers is excellent. They are quiet and print much faster than most other printers.

The quality of the output from laser printers is measured in terms of *resolution*. The resolution refers to the number of dots per inch (dpi) that the printer uses to produce the image. 600 dpi means that the printer prints 600 dots per inch horizontally by 600 dots per inch vertically. The more dots, the denser and better the image; the higher the dpi, the better the image.

Laser printers do not print one character at a time. They form the entire image and print that image all at once. Because of this, they require memory. As the information comes to them from the computer they must be able to "remember" what line 1 and line 2 look like while the computer goes on to feed them the information about line 3 and line 4, etc. One or two MB of memory is adequate if you are going to be printing mostly text. If you are going to be printing graphics on a regular basis, you should probably have at least four MB of memory in your laser printer.

The speed of laser printers, like that of ink jets, is measured in pages per minute. Obviously, the faster, the better. Who wants to wait around for that paper to come out of the printer?

Other Printers

Color laser printers with excellent output, are also available, although they are expensive. These and several other types of printers are used for special applications because of their higher costs.

Thermal wax color printers produce excellent images by using heated colored wax, melted in place onto the paper.

122

Thermal dye transfer printers, or dye sublimation printers, transform the ink into a gas which hardens on the page, producing high quality color images that look like photos.

Plotters use colored pens to draw detailed designs. These expensive printers are used primarily by architects, engineers and graphic designers.

One specialized printer that is both interesting and afford-able is the label printer. They are so small that you can hold them in one hand. Label printers were created especially for printing rolls of labels. This makes them ideal for printing large quantities of labels for mailings or for files. You can also print labels on any of the printers that were mentioned above. However, it is cumbersome to have to change the paper to label stock for just one or two labels. Also, if a label gets stuck inside a regular printer it can be very difficult to remove. So, the label printer fits an important niche.

Setting up Your Printer

In order to print the information that you have in your computer, the printer and computer must have a link. If the printer has an infrared port, information has to be sent between the computer and the printer without any physical connection. However, the most common way to create the necessary link between the printer and the computer is by using a cable. The cable does not usually come with the printer, so you will prob-ably have to purchase it separately. The connection to the computer is made through the computer's serial or parallel port. Most often the parallel port is used because it is able to transfer information faster than the serial port.

All printers receive their information from the computer. This requires a basic cable that is capable of sending informa-tion in only one direction, from the computer to the printer.

Many printers send communications from the printer to the computer, as well. They often send the computer information about their current status. For example, they are able to tell the computer when they are out of paper or ink. These printers will not work properly with the one-way cable. They require *a bi-directional* cable that permits the data to travel in both directions. Check with your printer manufacturer or look in your printer documentation to find out which type of cable you need. Or, buy a bi-directional cable, which will work in any circumstances.

When you purchase a cable you will have a choice of lengths. Keeping the printer close to the computer is important for easy accessibility. If you must keep the printer a slight distance away from the computer, that's perfectly all right. The normal printer cable is about twelve feet long. If you plan on purchasing a cable longer than that, check with your printer documentation or the manufacturer. Some printers will not work with longer cables.

After you connect the printer and the computer, the computer needs to know that you have attached a printer. You must give the computer information on how to run the printer

TIP

Remember—the disks that came with the printer are very important. You will need to have them if you ever want to move the printer to another computer. Be sure to keep them in a safe place with easy access.

that you have attached. This is done with a piece of software called a *print driver*. All printers come with a disk, or sometimes several disks, that contain the necessary print driver. Instructions for installing the print driver are also included with the printer. Just follow the instructions for installation. It is a simple step-by-step process.

Using Your Printer

The number of buttons or controls that you find on printers can vary greatly, however, there are two buttons that you find on almost all printers: the *form-feed* button, sometimes labeled "FF" and the *on-line* button. The form-feed button allows you to eject a paper from the printer. The on-line button is a toggle switch. Pressing this button alternates the printer between on-line and off-line. Most printers have a light that illuminates when the printer is on-line. On-line simply means that the printer is ready to receive communications from the computer. When you take the printer off-line, you temporarily take control of the printer to perform other functions, like using the form feed button. You must return the printer to the on-line status in order to give control of the printer back to the computer.

Printer Troubleshooting

When your printer doesn't seem to be working, first make sure that the printer is turned on and on-line. If it still doesn't work, check the cable and make sure that it is tightly connected on both ends. See your printer documentation for instructions on running a test page, called a *self-test*. Simply pressing a few buttons on the control panel usually does this. If the self-test doesn't print properly, you will know that you have a problem with the printer itself. If the self-test prints out properly, you will know that you have a problem with the cable, the computer software or the set up.

Each program you use needs to be told what printer you are using. Usually, the operating system does this for you. If, for example, you are using Windows 95, Windows tells each program which print driver to use. Sometimes, however this doesn't work, or gets messed up. You may have to tell the program which printer to use, yourself. If you are using Microsoft Word and are having trouble printing, check to make sure that the printer is set up properly. In Word, you would choose File from the menu and then choose Print. You will then see information about the printer that Word is using. You can change the printer here. If you choose the Properties button, you can change other print settings, as well.

If you find that you are not printing at all or are not printing correctly, and have checked the printer power and connections, reset the system. Exit your programs and your operating system properly. Then press the *reset button*, or turn the computer off, wait a minute or two and turn the computer back on again. Internal conflicts can sometimes cause the printer to become confused or erratic in its behavior. Resetting the system will reset all the print drivers and defaults, and often solve your printing problems.

Creative Printing

You don't have to limit yourself to printing boring letters and envelopes. With color ink jet printers you can design and print greeting cards, flyers, postcards, magnets and buttons. You can even decorate your own T-shirts with special T-shirt transfer paper. You create your design, print it out and iron it on the T-shirt. You

126

cannot make T-shirt transfers on a laser printer because it uses toner instead of ink.

Although your laser printer probably only prints in black and shades of gray, you can still produce some eye-catching documents. Colored paper stock is available from many sources. There are also several mail-order companies that offer special paper for creating brochures, business cards, certificates and presentations. The paper itself comes pre-printed with designs in various colors and design choices. Use your laser printer to add the black text. The results are often quite dramatic. The names of several paper suppliers that produce this type of paper are listed in the resource guide in the back of this book.

Scanners

When you want to put a picture or graphic into your computer, you need an input device called a *scanner*. A scanner is so-called because it scans an image, usually from a sheet of paper. The scanner then translates the information that it reads on the page into a format that the computer can understand. Once the image has been reproduced in the computer, you can change, edit or print it. For some people a scanner will be a necessity; for some, a luxury.

Hand-Held Scanners

An inexpensive option is the hand-held scanner. To scan text or an image into the computer, you slide the scanner sensor over the page that you want to duplicate.

There are several problems with these types of scanners. You need a steady hand to get a glitch-free image. Also, these units are only about 4" wide, so if you want to scan in an entire page, you have to scan it in strips that are pieced together by the computer.

The advantage to this type of scanner is that it can usually be hooked up to the parallel port on the computer. It provides a pass through, which enables you to use the same port for your printer. You do not have to open the computer to install any extra hardware with this type of scanner. It is good for importing small images, such as logos or small news clips, into your computer, but for anything larger you will find it extremely frustrating to use.

Some hand-held scanners can scan a whole page at a time. Some have rollers that let the scanner "walk" across the page automatically, eliminating the need for a steady hand.

Sheet-Feed Scanners

If you want an inexpensive way to scan pages of text and graphics into your computer, look at the scanners which I call *sheet-feed* or personal scanners. These scanners are generally 12-15" in width and vary in depth from 5" to about 10". They allow you to feed in single sheets of paper. They can also "walk across" the page, if the material that you want to copy is in a bond format, such as a book. Some scan only in black and shades of gray, while others scan in color. As with hand-held scanners, installation is usually easy and does not require you to open up your computer.

128

Flatbed Scanners

The best type of scanner is a flatbed scanner, if you want the best quality copy. You can scan in single pages, pages from books, scraps of paper, and even real-life objects. Flatbed scanners are used by all professional and industrial professionals, but they are also well-suited to home and small office use. These scanners are superior to the other types of scanners, even though they are quite large and take up considerable desktop space.

Most scanners of this type need to connect to a *SCSI* (Small Computer System Interface), (pronounced *skuzzy*) port. Since most computers don't have a port like this built in, (except for Macs), the scanner usually comes with its own SCSI interface card. You must open the computer and install this card before you can hook up the scanner. Installation of the card is simple, but getting the card and the scanner to work is not always easy. You might want to try to do this installation yourself. If it goes smoothly, you're home free. If you need help with the installation, you can call the manufacturer for technical support. Allow yourself plenty of time and to have a local professional available, just in case you need one.

Resolution Determines Quality

To determine the quality of images that a scanner will produce, you need to look at the scanner's *resolution*. The resolution refers to the amount of detail that the scanner can reproduce. The higher the resolution, the better the image quality. The resolution is measured in dots per inch or dpi. Sometimes you will see two types of resolution listed: *optical resolution* and *interpolated resolution*. It is easier to compare scanners if you just compare the optical resolutions. These are the same types of resolutions that are given when you look at the quality of output produced by a printer.

When you scan graphic images into the computer they take up a large amount of space on your hard disk. You can choose the resolution that the scanner will use, up to the maximum resolution of which the scanner is capable. However, if you use the maximum resolution, and do numerous scans, your hard disk will fill up quickly. If you plan to do extensive high-resolution scanning, you should plan on having extra disk space available.

Scanning in Color

Color scanners allow you to scan in photographs and other color documents. The number of colors that are processed determines the clarity and brilliance of the colors. You will see this represented by terms such as 8-bit, 24-bit and 30-bit color. For example, 24-bit color uses 16 million colors! If you plan to scan in pictures, manipulate them, and then send them to a professional printer, buy a 24-bit or 30-bit scanner. If you only want to view them on your screen and print them on an ink jet printer, even 24-bit color will produce more colors than your monitor or printer can display.

Software for Your Scanner

When you shop for a scanner you will find that they come with bundled software, just as many computers do. Sometimes the software that comes with the scanner will help you to make a decision about which scanner to purchase. In order to get the most out of your scanner you will need three programs: a program that allows you to scan in the image, one that does optical character recognition (text), and one that allows you to manipulate graphics.

Most scanners come with the software needed to scan in

images. This software is usually geared to the scanner and will work quite well with it.

Optical Character Recognition

If the image that you scanned in is text, you will probably want to be able to work with that text. Optical character recognition, or OCR software, allows the scanner to read handwritten or printed text and to convert that text into characters that the computer can understand. When you scan a page of text, it is just a bunch of lines and squiggles to the computer. The OCR program changes those lines and squiggles into the alphabetical and numerical characters and symbols. No program is able to do that with 100% efficiency, but the better programs today boast efficiencies of up to 98%. After you run the output from your scan through an OCR program, you are able to change or edit the text in any word processing program, just as if you had written it yourself on the computer. If you plan to scan newspaper articles, contracts or large amounts of text into your computer, you will need a good OCR program.

Graphics Software for Your Scanner

When you buy a good scanner you will want to scan in pictures as well as change and manipulate them. A good graphics program will allow you to do that. These programs vary greatly in what they can accomplish and also in the amount of time that you will have to invest in learning the program. For example, Adobe Photo-

131

shop, the granddaddy of all graphics programs, allows you to manipulate pictures in amazing ways. However, if you want to use Photoshop effectively you will need to invest a good deal of time in learning how to use the program.

Other Scanners

There are several other types of scanners that are quite interesting. Photo scanners are small desktop scanners that are made just for scanning photographs. Business card scanners will allow you to scan every business card that you acquire and will keep a database of names and addresses. Slide and film scanners are also available, but the audience for these is quite limited.

Digital Cameras

A digital camera allows you to take a picture without film. The picture is transferred directly from the camera to your computer. This technology is allowing newspapers and magazines to get their pictures into print even more quickly than before.

The price of digital photography continues to drop and has finally hit a level where many average home and business users can afford it. Everyone can use the same technology that allows professional photographers to get their photos printed quickly. With a digital camera you can take a picture and E-mail it to a relative or business associate. You could take a picture of your newborn baby in the morning, send it to grandma and grandpa, and they could see that photo the same afternoon. Now that's good use of technology!

A digital camera looks and acts just like a regular camera.

You shoot the picture in the usual way. Some of these cameras have a small LCD monitor, allowing you to preview the photograph after it's shot. If it turned out just as you had planned, you can keep the photo. If the picture wasn't as good as you had hoped, discard it and take another one. What a great feature for amateur photographers!

Many of the features of digital cameras are the same as those of non-digital cameras. They come with or without a built-in flash. Some have special lenses included or additional lenses available. The output is usually measured in the same type of resolution or dpi that we discussed earlier. Most cameras come with the cables and software necessary, but you should check on this before you make a purchase.

Another important detail to investigate with the digital camera is the output. The pictures that digital cameras produce vary in size. Also, some cameras have removable storage and some do not. A camera without removable storage will allow you to take a limited number of photographs. When the camera is full, you need to download the pictures to the computer to be able to take more photos. With removable storage, you can remove a small disk with the pictures on it and insert a new disk, and keep on taking pictures. Obviously, the second type of camera is preferable if you will be going on vacation and not taking your computer along.

The advantages of digital cameras are incredible. After you take a picture, you download it to your computer. When it appears on your computer screen you can use software to manipulate the image. You can remove the red eyes, improve the colors, change the background or remove unwanted portions of the picture. You can even put Aunt Edna's head on Aunt Jane's body, if you so desire. If you don't have a color printer or are not happy with the output from your printer, you can send the pictures on computer disk to be printed professionally. The advantage is that you only have to send in the pictures that you want to keep. This may be the answer to the drawers full of old photographs that most of us haven't had the time to organize. With digital cameras, photography can be a great hobby without the cost of having your own dark room.

The Video Connection

You can connect some digital cameras to your TV for viewing or you can copy the images onto videotape using your VCR. This allows you to create your own collage, or slide show, of images. There are also other devices that capture a video picture from your TV, camcorder, or VCR and turn them into a digital image in your computer. These devices are inexpensive and easy to use.

Some digital cameras have sound capabilities; some have full-motion video and sound.

Joysticks

People who use joysticks certainly know how to have fun with their computers. Joysticks are aptly named because they are used to play games on the computer. Joysticks are used to control objects in games. For example, if you are playing a pinball machine game, the joystick will move the paddles. If you are playing a shoot-em-up game, the joystick allows you to aim and shoot your guns. I am not a big game fan, but I am told that the most important thing about joysticks is their *feel*. The rule is try before you buy. Speaking of feel, there are joysticks that vibrate in certain ways, allowing you to "feel" what is happening on the screen. This is the beginning of the world of virtual reality that is bound to come.

Various joysticks have additional features. The type of games that you play the most might determine the features that you need on your joystick. For instance, there are joysticks that look like the yoke of an airplane. Obviously, this type of joystick is used by game enthusiasts who love to play flying games.

The most precise joysticks on the market are the digital/optical joysticks.

Many computers have a port that is used just for joysticks. It is usually marked "game." If your computer does not have a game port you can purchase an adapter and hook the joystick up to a serial port. If your computer does not have an empty serial port, you can buy a card to install inside your computer that will have a game port on it. Installation will be easy.

A Summary . . .

1. Experience your computer's power with additional equipment:

   - Printers:
     - dot-matrix
     - ink jet
     - laser.
   - Scanners:
     - hand-held
     - sheet-feed
     - flatbed.

2. Resolution of printers and scanners determine quality.

3. Have fun with digital cameras, video connections and joysticks.

The Ins and Outs of Buying Software

———◆———

Chapter 9

"The more alternatives, the more difficult the choice."

— *Léonor J.C. Soulas*

Free Software

What's the best type of software? Software that you don't have to pay for, of course. There are two types of software that are completely free of charge. *Public domain* software is information that you can get from the Internet or can copy from any other source without a fee involved. This type of software has no copyright restrictions and you can do whatever you like with it.

Freeware is another type of software that is free. You can copy or download it without having to pay anyone for it. Freeware differs from public domain software in that it is copyrighted. You can use it, but you can't sell it as your own.

Shareware

Shareware is another type of software. Many people think that shareware is free, but that is not true. Like freeware, shareware is copyrighted. You can download or copy shareware as you please. However, if you want to keep using the software after the trial period, usually one-month, you are expected to register the software with the creator and pay a fee for it. Some software will flash warnings on the screen to remind you to register after the trial period is over. Other software gives you no reminder and relies on the integrity of the user to pay the fee. One of the  reasons that shareware is so popular is that, in comparison to packaged software, it is usually inexpensive. Some shareware programs are as good as, or even better than, their shrink-wrapped counterparts. They can be sold more economically because shareware software has low advertising, marketing and distribution costs.

Beta Software

Some programs that appear to be free can have strings attached. This is the case with *Beta* software.

Developing software can be a complex process. Each section of code is written and tested and rewritten. When the entire program is completed, it still needs further testing.

The program first goes through Alpha testing, which is in-house testing by the software developer. When the company decides that the program is working fairly well, it goes into Beta testing. In Beta testing, the program is distributed to people outside the company. These people are able to use the program free of charge. In return, they are asked to report *bugs* or problems with the program to the company. A *bug* is anything in a program that doesn't work properly. The purpose of Beta testing is to find the small bugs in the program.

In today's wacky Internet world, Beta software is often made available for anyone to download. The company that created the software is betting that they will find out about bugs in this manner. They are letting the general public do the work that they should be doing.

There are two problems with Beta software. First, it can really screw up your system. Because this software, by definition, is not yet completely tested, it can conflict with other programs and cause major damage to your computer files. Secondly, companies do not provide technical support for Beta products. You will usually find a notice to that effect on the download page. However, some of these notices are very small and/or obscure. So, if you install the Beta release of a program on your computer, you are taking some chances. Even if the program has been released by a major software company, that company has no obligation to you if a problem does occur.

Buying Software

In order to be a smart software consumer you have to know why you are buying the software. Additionally, you need to choose software that will live up to your expectations. That sounds easy, but in reality it is sometimes a fairly difficult task.

Assess what type of program you need to buy. For example, do you need a word processing program, a personal information manager or a database? The information given in this chapter will help you make that decision. In some cases, these programs overlap. You will have to compare the features of several programs to make an intelligent decision.

After you decide what type of program you need, look at all the available programs of that type. Talk to friends and neighbors who are computer users. Ask what programs they use and see if they are happy with them. Most importantly, do a little research. Go to the store and compare the products. If the salesperson actually uses the product that he or she is selling, that person might be a good source of information. If, however, the salesperson has never actually used the program, don't take anything he/she says as gospel truth.

The Internet is a wonderful research tool to use when purchasing software. Access the company's home page to find information on the product that you are interested in. Often, you can download a demo version of the software to try before you buy. A demo is not Beta software. It is simply a trial version of the software.

When you get information from the manufacturer, remember that they will sometimes say whatever is necessary for you to buy their product. One of the best ways to research a software program is to read reviews in computer magazines. Again, you will find the Internet a useful tool as well.

Popularity

When choosing software, the popularity of the software can, and probably should, influence your decision. For instance, Microsoft Word has a large share of the word processor market for personal computers. *Word* has become popular because it is an excellent program. If Word has all the features that you need, the popularity of the program should make you want to purchase it over all of the others.

When one program dominates the market, it becomes the standard and carries additional advantages. For instance, more people will be able to share your files. If you change jobs, the computer programs that you know will most likely be the ones used by your new company.

Of course, there might be an overwhelming reason to buy a different program. You should not always feel obliged to purchase the most popular program. Just make sure that you include popularity as one of your criteria when you are shopping.

Versions

Be aware that different versions of a piece of software can vary greatly. For instance, CorelDraw Version 3 is an excellent product, stable and useable. When Corel updated this program they added many good features. But when CorelDraw 4 came out, it was a buggy, unstable program. Corel, an excellent company, quickly brought out CorelDraw 5 which corrected all the problems and added even more new features. Each newer version has been excellent, as well. The easiest way for the average user to determine the quality of a new version of a software program is to let someone else try it out first. As noted earlier, reading software reviews will save you time and money when making software choices.

Most software vendors number the versions or revisions sequentially, like the Corel products that we just mentioned — CorelDraw 3, CorelDraw 4, etc. Sometimes companies also distribute interim or smaller revisions. For instance, Microsoft's 3.0 version of Windows was not a very good program. Microsoft fixed the problems, and released a version called 3.1. They didn't call it 4.0 because it was not a full revision with added features; it was only what they considered an interim revision, so they called it version 3.1. This version was an excellent product and caught on with the public. Now few people are using Windows 3.0; most are using Windows 3.1.

In 1995, when Microsoft introduced their new version of Windows, they called it Windows 95 instead of Windows 4.0. Doing that allowed consumers to know how old a program was by the name, indicated by the year the product was introduced. This also offered Microsoft a new marketing tool: they could create increased demand for the latest version.

Another product that software developers have created is a *light* or *lite version* of their software. A light version is a pared-down version of the original software package. The core product is left untouched, but many of the extras have been removed. Some light versions are sold as stand-alone packages, but many are bundled with hardware. If you buy a scanner, you might get a copy of a graphics program called Photoshop Lite. The software developer is expecting that you will like the program and will want to upgrade to the full version to receive the additional features that were removed. Of course, there is always a fee involved in upgrading to the full version.

A *suite* of programs is a group of software by one manufacturer. You can often get upgrade pricing or competitive upgrade pricing even if you only own one program that is a part of the suite. For example, if you own an old version of Word, you are eligible for the upgrade price of Microsoft Office, which includes Word and several other programs. The upgrade pricing offers you considerable savings over the full-version pricing, so be sure to check this out.

Upgrades

If you have registered your software, the software company will notify you when a new version of their product is released. At that time, they will offer to let you purchase the new version, which is considered an *upgrade*, at a discount.

In some cases, you can also get a reduction in price by buying what is called a *competitive upgrade*. If you own a competitor's product, many companies will offer you a reduced price. If, for instance, you decide that you want to update your word processing software from WordPerfect to Microsoft Word or Lotus' Word Pro, you are eligible to purchase a competitive upgrade. Either Microsoft or Lotus will be happy to give you this price reduction to steal you away from WordPerfect. The competitive upgrade pricing works with many different types of programs, such as spreadsheets, drawing programs and databases. Check with the manufacturer of the product that you are going to purchase for details.

When a new version of the software that you are using comes on the market you have to decide whether or not that new version will offer you enough additional new features to be worth the price. Review the new features through the company's marketing literature or on the Internet at the company's home page. You can call the company and have them fax you a list or give you the information over the phone. If there are two or more features that you would use consistently, consider purchasing the upgrade.

Software vendors are pressured to release products as quickly as possible. Thus, they often release software and deal with the bugs later. When enough customers call customer support to complain about a certain problem with the program, the company fixes the problem or the bug, with what is called a *patch*. A patch is a small series of instructions that are used to fix a programming bug. It is called a patch because the original programming code stays in place and the code, or instructions that fix the problem are added like an overlay.

Patches are given to a customer when he calls technical support with a problem. They can be copied from the Internet or a bulletin board, or can be sent to you on a floppy disk. Some major programs have hundreds of patches. These patches are often grouped together and become a new mini version, like Program Version 1a, or Program Version 1.12. Sometimes the patches, like those for Windows 95, become what is called a *service release*. There is often a fee for these upgraded versions.

Complain, Complain, Complain

Sooner or later, the software industry will become more responsive to the consumer. It is hard to believe that any industry could put out products that don't work properly and not be flooded with calls from irate customers. Having a programming background, I certainly understand the complexity of software. I also understand that these programs are run on many different makes and models of computers, creating large number of variables that need to be considered by the manufacturers. Customer service and product performance has reached a level that I believe to be unbearable.

Computer software customers wait for hours to get in touch with technical support. When they finally do reach a technician, they are told that there is a fix available to *their* problem. Then the customer must spend more time logging onto the Internet and downloading the patches and spend even more time installing them on his or her computer. Often, he has to do this several times for the same program. In some cases, the customer is even required to pay for the fixes.

I recently purchased a new program from one of the major software suppliers in the industry. When I tried to install the program I found that one of the floppy disks was bad. I called customer service to get a new disk. They had me call technical support to make sure that I needed a new disk. I waited forty-five minutes to get through to technical support. Technical support said I needed a new disk and told me to call customer service back. Customer service then told me that they would gladly send me a new disk at no charge. I would only have to pay $9.95 for shipping and handling. They had sent me a defective product and then expected me to pay an extra fee to rectify the situation. I am telling this story because it is typical of the software industry today.

The only weapon we have to overcome this situation is to express our dissatisfaction. Call, write, or E-mail. Whatever method you choose, make sure that when you are dissatisfied, each and every company knows about it.

Software Licenses

A software license agreement is a legal agreement between the end user (licensee) and the software developer. It sets the terms and conditions under which that software may be legally used. Many programs will show you the license agreement when you install the program and ask you to click a button showing that you accept the stated terms. The license agreement can also be found with the program's written documentation. Purchasers do not seem to take the time to actually read the agreements, but if they did they would find them interesting.

License agreements allow you to make a backup copy of the software for archival purposes only. With many programs, you are allowed to use one copy of the software per computer. You violate the license agreement and break the law if you install that software on more than one computer, even if you are the owner of all of the computers in question.

Some companies provide flexibility by allowing some kind of concurrent use. For instance, a license agreement for one large software vendor says the following: "If you have a stand-alone copy of one of our software titles, and it is installed and used by you 80 percent of the time on your office computer, you may use that copy at home provided you are the only user of that software. (No simultaneous usage is permitted.) Other users must purchase and use their own copy of the software."

The company that I just quoted actually put the license information into terms that the average user can understand. Unfortunately, the license agreements from many software vendors are written in such complex legal terms that they are indecipherable to the average person. In one case, I had to call a software manufacturer to ask for an explanation of what their license agreement really meant. I hope that software companies will make these agreements easier to understand in the future.

If you copy software in violation of the license agreement and give it to your friends or colleagues, or if you purchase one copy of such software and use it on three computers at your office, you are committing *software piracy*. Unauthorized copying, or software piracy, costs the software industry billions of dollars each year. It harms all software companies and eventually harms the user as well. If we could end this practice, software companies could use their newly found revenue to invest in research and development, preventing some of the program defects that plague software. We, personally, can do little to prevent software piracy in other countries, but we can have an effect on piracy here at home.

Returning Software

Whether or not you are able to return software depends on where you purchased it. Some stores or mail-order companies will allow you to return software for any reason, even if

146

you just don't like it. Others will not let you return software for any reason. There are many variations between these two extremes. Be sure to check out the return policy before you buy any software.

Some manufacturers offer their own satisfaction guarantee. They allow you to try the software for a certain period of time, usually 30 days. If you don't like it, they will refund your money. If you are unable to return it to where you bought it, you can still return it directly to the manufacturer. Such a transaction takes a little longer, but it is better than keeping a program you will never use.

Some software vendors allow you to download a demo of their product from the Internet. This is usually a full version of the software that you can use for a certain period of time before you are required to pay for it. This is similar to shareware, but is more expensive. This is a great way to try a program before you buy. Most of the companies that offer this type of trial usage have written code into the demo programs that makes it unusable after the trial period has expired. This forces the user to pay for the program if they want to continue using it. In any case, this is an easy way to test drive a piece of software.

TIP
Turn off your screen saver and any other programs that may be running, before you install a new program.

Installing Software

Installing new software simply means copying the application from floppy disks, or CD-ROMs, to your hard disk. When you are ready to begin this process you will need to find the *installation disk*, which is usually marked installation disk, or *Disk #1*. If the program came on CD-ROM, the installation program will be on the CD. Read the instructions that came with the program. They will usually tell you to insert the disk or CD and type a simple instruction into the computer. For example, if you are working in Windows 95, the instructions might say: "Insert the program disk, open the *Start* menu and select *Run*. Then type *X:\ setup*, where X is the drive where you inserted the disk."

This is confusing to some new computer users, but it is actually quite simple.

- Your floppy disk will be either Drive A or Drive B. In most cases it will be Drive A.

- Your hard disk is drive C. Sometimes your hard disk is broken up into two parts. In which case, it will be drives C & D.

- Your CD-ROM will usually be Drive D or Drive E.

You can confirm the exact drive specification by looking in "my computer" where you will see a graphic representation of each drive. (If you are using Windows 3.1, look in *file manager.*)

Make sure that you type in the instruction as stipulated in the directions, including all colons and slashes. After you type this and press *enter*, the installation program will take over. It may ask you to answer some questions, such as your name and address. The installation program may also ask questions like: Where do you want to install the program? If you don't know the answer or don't understand the question, just press the enter key and the computer will use the *default*, or most commonly used settings.

Some CD-ROM programs give you two installation options.

Option 1: You can install the entire program to the hard disk. This will make the program run faster, but will take up more hard disk space.

Option 2: You can install only part of the program on the hard disk. This will save disk space, but the program will run more slowly. If you choose this option, the CD-ROM must be in the drive for the program to run.

A Summary . . .

Software comes in many packages. Get the most out of the software you purchase by knowing about:

- Shareware and freeware
- Demo and Beta programs
- How to qualify for upgrades
- Software bugs and patches
- What software licenses really mean
- How to install new software

Software That Gets Down to Business

---◆---

Chapter 10

*"I like work; it fascinates me.
I can sit and look at it for hours."*

— Jerome K. Jerome

Software Suites

A suite is a group of programs that are sold together. This format is becoming a popular way to distribute software because it offers substantial savings. If you were to purchase each of the applications in the suite separately, you would pay much more. Packaging programs in this manner is also advantageous to the manufacturer. They are able to use the suite to get more of their programs distributed, which helps those programs become even more popular. Once a program has a large market share, people will purchase it just because it is the most popular and most recognizable program of its kind.

When suites were first introduced, some manufacturers would include one or two good programs along with several others that were not so good. Fortunately for the software users, there are now several suites available which contain a complete set of excellent programs.

The user gains another benefit when he purchases a software suite. The programs in a suite are usually *integrated*. This means that they are able to work together and share information easily. Some suites offer better integration than others. Manufacturers are realizing that this feature is important to the user and are increasing the integration of their products.

One other nice feature about a well-written and well-integrated suite of programs is that they all will work in a similar manner. Once you have learned to use one program, you will be able to apply the same methods to every other program in the suite. This cuts down learning time.

Sometimes suites are offered in different configurations. For instance, the standard edition of a suite might have four programs in it. The professional edition will have the same four programs with an additional program. The home, and/or small office edition, might contain four different programs. All you have to do is to choose the edition that is best suited to your needs.

License agreements also pertain to suites. You will find that many license agreements prohibit the breaking up of these suites. If you purchase a suite of programs, it may be illegal to install the word processing program on your computer and give the spreadsheet program to your neighbor, even if you do not install the spreadsheet program on your computer.

Word Processing Programs

In 1908, Henry Ford cranked up his first Model A Ford. For years people routinely cranked up their cars to get them started. Then one day the automatic starter was invented, and from that time on, no one wanted to mess around with those old cranking mechanisms anymore.

The relationship between the typewriter and a computer equipped with a word processing program is similar. However, when you see what a word processor can do, you no longer want to use a typewriter. In fact, in most offices, the typewriter has become obsolete. Word processing programs are the most widely used computer applications. They, alone, have put computers on desks around the world.

TIP

You will find a recommended software section in the back of this book to help you in selecting the software that best suits your needs.

The Basics

Word processing programs allow you make changes to a document without having to retype or redo the entire document. Because of this fact alone, they avoid wasted time and increase productivity. They also give you editing and formatting features that help you produce professional looking documents.

Word processing allows the process of creating the document to be separated from the process of printing the document. You are able to edit, change and alter the document before you print it. You can also be bolder in trying new ideas, knowing that if you don't like what you have done you can change your mind, without having committed yourself to paper. When used with the right attitude, a word processing program can help a person to be much more creative than he could ever be with a typewriter.

A word processing program moves from line to line for you. You just type in the text without any concern for where you are on a line. You do not have to press return at the end of a line. The computer knows when you reach the end of the line and it automatically goes to the next line. The computer also automatically hyphenates words at the end of a line. This certainly makes producing documents easier.

Understanding Fonts

There are several terms that you will need to understand when you begin using a word processing program. The first of these is the word *font*. A font consists of three elements: the typeface, the type size and the type style.

The typeface refers to the design of the characters. For example, you might use a typeface called Times New Roman, a typeface which is used by many newspapers and in most office correspondence. If you want your document to have a more informal look you might choose a typeface like *Brush Script*, which will give the characters a handwritten look.

After you choose the typeface, decide how big you would like your type to be. This is referred to as the type size. The size of the characters is measured in *points*. There are approximately 72 points to an inch. Most business documents use 10 or 12 point type.

The last element of a font is the type style. Some examples of different type styles are **bold**, *italic* and <u>underline</u>. This paragraph of text, for example, is 12 point Times New Roman.

When you use a word processor, you can change the typeface, style or size by clicking the mouse on your choice. This gives your documents a more finished and professional look.

Formatting a Document

Word processing programs also allow you to make choices regarding how your page will look. This is called page *formatting* and can usually be done by choosing *File* and the *Page Setup* from your word processor's menu. You can specify the margins that you would like to use, and the paper size and *orientation*. Paper orientation defines whether the page will be printed in a vertical or horizontal mode.

There are many other choices when creating a document. You can create your page with more than one column. Page numbers and *headers* and *footers* can be added to your document. A header is information, or a graphic at the top of the page. A footer is information at the bottom of the page. You can set tabs and create *bulleted* and numbered lists easily. A bulleted list precedes each item with an enlarged dot or other symbol. If you are new to word processing, don't let all these choices scare you. Many programs have what they call *Wizards* or other types of helpers that pop up on your screen to walk you through many of these tasks.

One of the best features of word processing programs is the spell-checker. Many programs also have an auto-correct feature that can correct typos and misspellings as you make them. I didn't win any spelling bees when I was in school, so this feature is a real godsend to me.

Word Processing Special Features

Word processors have many other special features. I will give you just a few of them here.

A document can be set up as a *template*. A template is a document that is designed to be used repeatedly as a pattern. It is opened as a copy of the original, allowing changes to be made to the copy, but not to the original. This can save considerable formatting and typing time on form letters and other often-used documents.

Search and Replace is a feature that allows you to find words, phrases or symbols and replace them with whatever you like. For example in a legal document the term "buyer" might be repeated several times. When the buyer's name is determined, the computer can find all the places where the word "buyer" appears, and replace it with the buyer's actual name. The replacement is made automatically.

Mail merge is a feature that allows you to create personalized letters, envelopes and mailing labels for each person on a mailing list. This feature is heavily used by offices for customer mailings, but even home users find it useful for mailing things such as Christmas cards and invitations.

Word processing programs today also allow you to insert graphics into your documents. You can also insert objects from other programs, such as spreadsheets or photos. This flexibility allows you to produce newsletters and brochures as well as reports and manuals.

Spreadsheets

A spreadsheet is a grid of columns and rows into which you enter information, usually numerical. In the late '70s Dan Bricklin and Bob Frankston created VisiCalc, the first electronic spreadsheet for the Apple II computer. It was responsible for much of Apple's early success.

The computer and the spreadsheet were a marriage made in heaven. The spreadsheet's structure allows the computer to be a number cruncher, and allows the data to be formatted in an understandable way. Spreadsheets are used for everything from adding simple rows of numbers to performing complex mathematical computations. The average user finds spreadsheet programs indispensable for personal and business financial calculations and reports.

In a spreadsheet, each box in the grid is called a *cell*. Each cell has an address, which defines its location on the spreadsheet. The rows are labeled numerically and the columns are labeled alphabetically. Cell B-5 will be at the intersection of the second column and the fifth row. Most spreadsheets can have more than two million cells. You don't have to worry about running out of space.

The user usually fills in the grid of cells with pertinent numbers. He or she also writes the formulas that tell the spreadsheet how to produce the proper results. The spreadsheet then performs all the calculations. If you change one number in a cell, the program will recalculate the entire spreadsheet to reflect that change.

For instance, if you formulate a spreadsheet to determine the amount of interest you will pay on a loan at prime rate, when the prime rate changes you only have to change one number. All the payment information is updated automatically.

This feature is useful for *what-if* analysis. You can insert different numbers to simulate several possible scenarios. For example, what if the prime rate went up to 20%? What if the prime rate dropped to 2%?

When you view a large spreadsheet on the screen you will see only a portion of the entire sheet. Use the arrow keys or click the mouse on the scroll button to see the rest.

The main function of a spreadsheet is to do mathematical calculations. Spreadsheets have ready-to-use formulas, called *functions*, that allow you to perform calculations without having to type in long, complex formulas. For example, the computer will understand terms such as *sum*, *average*, *minimum* and *maximum*.

You might have seen the output from early computer spreadsheets: rows and columns of tiny numbers printed on large green and white striped sheets of paper. Striped paper was used to help you keep track of which numbers were in which row.

We've come a long way since those types of data sheets. You can add lines, shading and color to spreadsheets to make them more readable. You can easily format numbers to change their appearance, having the computer add dollar signs, commas or percent signs as needed. You can even change fonts to emphasize certain text and to make data easier to read.

Spreadsheets are intelligent. If, for example, you type in the words Monday and Tuesday and drag the mouse across several columns after that, the computer will fill in Wednesday, Thursday and Friday. If you do the same with the numbers 1 and 2, it will fill in 3,4,5, etc. If you type Mon. and Tues., it will fill in Wed., Thurs., and Fri. If you type in 5 and 10. It will fill in 15, 20 25, etc. The program will try to anticipate what you want.

Spreadsheets also have a built-in charting feature. If you create a small spreadsheet for your monthly expenses, you can turn that spreadsheet into a chart with the click of a mouse. You can even choose what type of chart you want—a bar graph or a pie chart.

Databases

A *database* is simply a collection of information. Database programs allow you to organize and retrieve that information. Some examples of databases are mailing lists, catalogues of products and address books. A good database program will sort, manipulate and analyze the data; create mailing labels, letters and envelopes; or create reports.

In a database, each collection of data is referred to as a *table*. So, for example, if you were creating a database listing all of the entries in your address book, all of the entries together would be a table.

Each individual entry is called a *record*. In our address book example, each person would have his/her own record. That person's address and telephone number and all related information would be a part of his record.

Each entry in a record is called a *field*. So in our address book example, each person's name would be a field. The home telephone number would be in a different field.

There are two types of databases. *Flat databases* contain only one table and the information in that table is not shared with any other tables. A *relational database* contains two or more tables that share common information. Our address book example is a flat database. However, if we decided to include climate information on the cities in our address book, we would create another table, which would list the name of the city and the climate information. Then, we have created a relational database. The information in our weather table relates to our name and address table because it has a common field—the city.

Flat databases are easy to set up; relational databases are more complex. Many businesses use relational databases to track their customers, inventories and orders and to see how they relate to each other. For example, they can easily see which customers have ordered various items in their inventory.

Database programs are customizable. With the proper setup a doctor's office can use the same database program that an automotive parts supplier might use. If the application is small and easy, anyone can customize a database program to suit special needs. However, if the data that needs to be tracked is complex, a computer professional is usually hired.

Presentation Software

Presentation software is used to create materials that are used in presentations, such as sheets to be presented in a  sequence, overhead transparencies or slides. Sometimes the presentations are shown on the computer screen or are transmitted to a projector screen. The simplest presentation software is a word processor. Dedicated presentation software, such as Microsoft Power Point or Lotus Freelance, gives you many extra features that make presentations quite simple.

These features include the ability to link and time screens to create slide shows. You can also include graphics, notes, animation and sound. Most of these applications allow you to create a presentation and publish it on the Internet.

Personal Information Managers

The most common database application is the personal address book. There are several inexpensive programs that offer a database customized for names and addresses. This saves you the trouble of purchasing a database program and customizing it yourself. As software companies compete for a broader share of the market, they have added extra features to their address book programs such as the ability to track *to-do* lists, or to have your computer automatically call phone numbers.

Then they combined a calendar and appointment-scheduling program with an address book program. A totally new type of program was born. We call these programs *personal information managers* or PIMs .

The address book section of a PIM is often called a *contact manager* because it does more that just give you a list of names and addresses. It can also keep track of when you contacted your friends or business associates and how long you talked to them. If you need to keep track of your contacts for business purposes, a full-blown contact management program will have numerous additional features.

The appointment and calendar sections of the personal information managers are useful for anyone who needs to keep track of their time or appointments. It can also help you schedule recurring events. For example, when you enter your mother's birthday, you tell the computer that this event will occur not just this year but every year. The computer will put it in your schedule every year. You can even have the computer notify you in advance of an event. You might want the computer to sound an alarm of some type one half-hour before an important meeting. If you want to be reminded to send your mother a birthday card, just set an alarm to go off a few days before her birthday.

Every PIM available today seems to have some unique features. Here are a few of the features available.

- Transfer address book information automatically to your word processor when you want to write a letter
- Access your E-mail and send E-mail directly from your PIM
- Calendar with group scheduling
- Document Management
- Tracking of time for billing purposes
- Manage projects

Personal information managers are useful programs that can save you time and increase your efficiency. The trick is to find one that you like. A PIM can be the hardest type of software to choose since everyone has a different style of working and organizing information. Different PIMs offer different features and ways of organizing information.

The best way to find a personal information manager that suits your needs is to try before you buy. There are also some shareware PIMs that are great. If you are looking at a commercial product, get a demo of the program, if you can. Other options include: find a store where you can try out the program, or ask a friend to let you see how their program works.

Money Managers

After you get your appointments in order, your address book complete and your *to do* list up-to-date you should feel much more organized. Your next step might be to get a program that helps you manage your money. For those of you who are now thinking that you don't have any money, let the computer help you budget your funds and find ways to save money.

Checkbook programs are excellent tools for money management and checkbook reconciliation. There are other features available in checkbook programs as well, including excellent report writing and charting, and investment tracking. Some have sections for home inventory and insurance information.

A checkbook program allows you to set up a detailed budget. Then, every time you write a check, you allocate that amount to a budget account or category. At the end of the month, or other time period of your choosing, you can compare your budgeted amounts and your actual amounts. You can even turn your spending trends into colorful charts. If nothing else, this might be one way to brighten up your financial picture.

You can also purchase customized checks that print directly from your checkbook program. This is an exciting feature for many folks who don't like to write out checks.

On-line banking is another great feature that you can use. This allows you to pay your bills directly from your account without writing a check. If you want to set up on-line banking, check with your bank first. Your bank might be limited to using only one program which you will need in order to bank on-line.

You can also sign up for a credit card that will download your transactions directly into your checkbook program. This allows you to manage your money without much hassle. Certain credit cards only work with certain programs, and there is an additional fee attached.

Investment Tracking

Many checkbook programs have some sort of investment tracking built-in. If you are buying a checkbook program for the purpose of tracking investments, be sure to look carefully at the features that are offered since they vary greatly from program to program.

If you have extensive investments, you might want to purchase a program that is dedicated to such transactions. Most of these programs offer on-line access for stock quotations. Most can be set up to automatically watch the stocks of your choosing. Some will alert you when the stock is outside the parameters that you set.

You can also make investment purchases on-line. Charges for on-line transactions vary greatly. Investigate this before you make a decision on which package to purchase.

Accounting

If you need to keep better track of your financial transactions than simple budgeting and check tracking, you will want to look at full-fledged accounting programs. Accounting programs and their prices vary greatly. You can buy an accounting program for $50 or you can spend $50,000. There are several inexpensive programs made especially for home and small businesses. These include things such as general ledger, checkbook, invoicing, and reporting. Many have extra features that include bids, inventory and job costing, contact management and custom forms.

The main difference in these programs is often ease of use. Some programs are written more from the accounting angle. If you have an accounting background, you will probably find that these programs make more sense to you and are easier to use. If you have absolutely no understanding of accounting, don't worry. There are several very good programs that were written with you in mind.

Often the most difficult part of using an accounting program is setting it up to suit your needs. Many programs will walk you through the set-up process step-by-step, offering help along the way. They use everyday terms and do a good job of handling your accounting needs.

If you use an accountant, always check with him or her before you purchase an accounting program. Most programs have reporting capabilities that are sufficient for the average user and the average accountant. However, if your accountant prefers working with the output from a certain program, his preference will certainly be influential in deciding which program to purchase.

You will also find that several programs have a feature that will allow your accountant to make changes to your data at his or her office and then merge them into your data. This allows you to continue working while your accountant is also working on your books.

Tax Programs

You can quickly compute your taxes on your computer

and with the click of a mouse, send your forms to the IRS. If you have kept good records during the year, it can be that easy. Be sure to purchase a tax program that works with your checkbook program. Also, be aware that you must buy a new tax program, or at least upgrade your program, every year, as these programs are rewritten each year to reflect the changes in the tax laws.

"Old minds are like old horses; you must exercise them if you wish to keep them in working order."

—John Quincy Adams

Educational Opportunities

I believe that this quote is true not just for old minds, but for any minds. We all need to stimulate our thought processes in order to keep them working properly. The computer is an extraordinary instrument. It presents us with information in many different forms, all of which can help us keep our minds active.

Computers can do the thinking for us, if we let them, but they can also be used to expand our creative talents and to help us amass the knowledge that we need to improve our lives.

With the computer you don't have to leave your desk. The world of education has come to you.

You can enroll in college classes over the Internet, investigate the hobby that you've been tinkering in, or use your computer for some serious research into any subject. The Internet gives you instant access to information

165

around the world. You can access everything from the Library of Congress to the Louvre. Who could ask for more food for the mind?

Learn a Language

There are also software programs that address the many aspects of learning. A great way to expand your mind is to learn a foreign language. Try to find a program that allows you to practice the language by recording your pronunciation of a word or phrase and comparing it to the correct pronunciation. You will need a microphone do to this, but they are quite inexpensive. Several language programs come with a microphone.

"The mind grows by what it feeds on."

— Josiah Gilbert Holland

Encyclopedias

Even with the resources available on the Internet, you will probably want to purchase several computer reference programs for regular use. The first of these should be a good encyclopedia. I remember the time, not too long ago, when you would have to pay a thousand dollars or more to have a good encyclopedia in your home. Now, you can have a full encyclopedia on CD-ROM for quite a bit less than one hundred dollars. These encyclopedias don't look as good as the old ones on the bookshelf, but offer several advantages, including multimedia functions, such as sound and video clips. You can hear and see Martin Luther King making his famous speech. You can listen to a harpsichord to find out what it actually sounds like. You can see and hear the action as the deciding play is made in the Super Bowl.

When you use a standard encyclopedia, you sometimes have to go from book to book looking for different occurrences of the subject that you are interested in. With a CD-ROM encyclopedias, you don't have to do any book shuffling. You type in the subject and a click of the mouse takes you to all of the areas that you need. If you have Internet access, you can use *hot links* that are listed in the encyclopedia. Hot links take you directly to related resources on the Internet. A click of the mouse can take you to a research facility halfway around the world, which specializes in the subject you have entered.

To keep your standard encyclopedia up-to-date, you had to purchase an annual yearbook. To research something, you had to look in each yearbook separately. Computerized encyclopedias make life much easier. You can download updated information monthly, if you like. Many encyclopedias are offered on a subscription basis. Each year they send you, for a moderate fee, a whole new updated encyclopedia. This is a first-rate value.

CD-ROM encyclopedias vary as much in content as their written counterparts. Some are geared toward the serious researcher while others are specifically targeted to younger age groups. Some have a high multimedia content and others have almost none.

Other Reference Books

I believe that no home or office should be without a good dictionary. You will find that most computerized dictionaries come on a CD-ROM. Because a CD-ROM can hold the contents of many books, dictionaries are usually found with some other grouping of reference books, such as a dictionary, thesaurus, atlas, almanac and book of quotations. Reference books are easy to use on the computer because they allow you to search for the information quickly and easily.

The *interface* that is used for reference books is important because this is the way the computer user interacts or communicates with the computer. If the interface is easy to use, the reference book becomes much more valuable.

Many people also find that having a medical encyclopedia in the house is a valuable resource. Like other reference books, medical books can take full advantage of the computer to extend our learning with graphics and other multimedia.

Utility Programs

Your computer uses utility programs to make it work better in some manner. Utilities will eventually be part of the operating system. In the meantime, we have to purchase them separately unless you are an Apple/Mac user. Some of the utilities that we will be talking about here are built into the Mac operating system.

Several utility programs available help you diagnose problems with your system when they occur. Some of them even prevent problems. Many of these programs offer diagnostic testing of your system hardware. One of the most difficult things in diagnosing problems is determining whether the hardware or the software is causing the problem. A diagnostic program can help you pinpoint the problem.

Utility programs can also help you recover files that you have accidentally erased or files that have become corrupted. Keep in mind that for these programs to work effectively, you must install them and have them running before the problem occurs.

Many utility programs run unobtrusively in the background. They keep track of your files, your hard disk and your other hardware, and monitor your system. Some of them also scan for viruses. They can tell you when you need to defragment your hard drive and can do it for you automatically.

Several of these programs allow you to make a recovery disk, or bootable system disk. The recovery or start-up disks that these programs make are superior to the start-up disk that you might make for your system. They have built in instructions that walk you through the restoration process and can automatically fix many common problems.

Like a good virus checker, a comprehensive utility program, like Norton Utilities, is a good insurance policy for your computer. It is not as necessary as a virus protection program, but if something does go wrong, you will be glad that you have one installed. Although programs like this are easy to use, you will have to learn how it works. Investigate the features of the program before you lose a file or need to use the diagnostics for troubleshooting.

Some programs perform only one of the tasks mentioned and some can do them all. I recommend finding a program that is as all-inclusive as possible.

Data Compression

One utility that has been incorporated into the operating system, at least on Windows systems, is *data compression.*

Data compression is a technique that saves space by removing empty fields, gaps and other unnecessary data on your hard disk. This is done by translating a file into a special coded format. Some files can be compressed more than others, but it is not unusual for the new file to be about one half the size of the old one.

One of the best reasons to compress a file is to save room on a hard disk. No matter how big your hard disk is, you always seem to run out of space, even if you remove old unwanted files and programs.

With DOS and pre-Windows 95 computers, you had to buy a special utility program to institute a data compression scheme. With Windows 95 you can use a built-in utility called Double Space. In either case, once you install data compression, it will run automatically in the background. The files will compress and decompress when you use them.

Since the files are constantly being compressed and decompressed, you may notice that your system is a little slower after you have installed data compression. Don't use data compression unless you have to.

To Install or Uninstall, That is the Question

Another type of utility program is the *uninstaller*. In the past, you could remove a program just by erasing the program's directory and files. Then Windows came on the scene. When you install a Windows program, that program writes files to its own directory, and also to many Windows directories. There are also many files that are shared by various Windows applications. When you decide to erase a Windows program, little scraps of information can remain on your hard disk in many different locations. All these scraps take up space on your hard disk. These pieces of data can also interfere with other programs. Uninstall programs were invented to alleviate this situation. If you are using Windows 3.1, you probably should use an uninstall program.

If you are using Windows 95, you need to read a little further. Windows 95 is a 32-bit operating system. This basically means that information can be transferred within the computer system 32-bits at a time. Older versions of the Windows operating system are 16-bit operating systems. In order to be compatible with older software, Windows 95 runs 16-bit software as well as 32-bit software. When Windows 95 was introduced, Microsoft built an uninstall program into the operating system. However, the built-in uninstall works only for 32-bit programs. So if you add a 32-bit program to your Windows 95 computer, you can uninstall it easily within Windows 95 itself. However, if you run any 16-bit software, and most of us will, you will still have to purchase an uninstall program to remove those programs.

One caveat here. You must purchase an uninstall program that is specifically written for your operating system. So, if you use Windows 3.1, buy a program that is specifically for Windows 3.1 systems. The same holds true for Windows 95 systems. If you use the wrong program for your operating system, you can mess up your hard disk.

Our Mac friends are lucky here. Most Apple/Mac program installers also uninstall or remove the programs as well. Now, that's the way it should be.

Uninstall programs work well most of the time, but I have seen occasions when they accidentally removed a file that was necessary for another program or for the operating system. Because of this, you should always backup your hard disk before you attempt to use these programs. Many people worry unnecessarily about removing programs. If you have room on your hard disk, don't worry about removing a program that you are not using anymore. It probably won't hurt anything. When your hard disk starts to fill up, it's time to think about a thorough cleaning.

171

A Summary...

1. Software suites offer value and integration.

2. Software can keep you organized, productive and efficient. Basic types include:

    - Word Processing

    - Spreadsheets

    - Databases

    - Presentation Software

    - Personal Information Managers

    - Money Management and Investment

    - Accounting and Tax Programs

    - Educational Programs

    - Reference Programs

Having Fun With Your Computer

Chapter 11

"All animals, except man, know that the principal business of life is to enjoy it."

— *Samuel Butler*

Radio and television are primarily for entertainment. You can, of course, also use both the radio and television to gather information and learn. However, the computer is truly a multi-functional machine in that respect. It is equally valuable for both serious and playful endeavors. Without a doubt, the computer can help us to be more productive and have more fun.

Action/Adventure Games

Games, games, games . . . . With a computer the choices are seemingly endless. Interactive is the keyword. The computer allows a user and a computer to communicate with, and respond to, each other. With each new technological advance, we come closer to creating true inter-activity with the computer. This is referred to as *virtual reality*. Advances with the Pentium MMX chip and three-dimensional graphics cards have made games more realistic than ever before.

The most popular games today are the action/adventure games. Most of these are in a category that I call shoot-em-up games. Even if you are not shooting guns, you always seem to

173

be shooting something. If you are past your teenage years, you will probably find that the manual dexterity required to play these games can be quite a challenge, but you might love them anyway.

The variety of games available is almost overwhelming. You can be in the air, in outer space, underwater, in a foreign land or right next door. You can be waging a bloody battle against alien invaders or knocking cute little pac-man-like characters off a fence. The graphics and sound built into these games can be exceptional. It's easy to be drawn into the action and there's no doubt about it, these games can be addictive.

If you are a game addict, upgrading to the newest 3-D technology will be more than worth your while. Be sure to purchase a good video board and joystick to make your gaming adventures most enjoyable.

Older DOS-based games had many memory problems and were often difficult to set up. Even when we moved to Windows, games were still often a problem. Windows 95 solved many of the memory problems. You can run most DOS-based games under Windows 95 without problems.

Be a Good Sport

With television, you can enjoy many sports from a comfortable chair in your living room. With a computer, no matter what your sport, you can enjoy it, play it, or learn about it without leaving home. The computer puts you right in the game. You can play basketball, football, baseball or golf. You can even go fishing on your computer screen.

If you choose a team sport, many programs enable you to create a *dream team*. For example, if baseball is your game, you could pit Babe Ruth against Sandy Koufax and fill in the rest of your team from a choice of other great players. This could be very exciting stuff for baseball fans.

Some games are well-suited to the computer. Take pool, for example. The computer displays the geometric angles of the game, allowing you to improve your skills. You can play golf on the computer and learn what club to use and also learn the rules of the game. Playing golf on the computer is exciting because you can travel around the world playing various golf courses. You will find the layouts and photography realistic. In fact, you can buy a golf program before your vacation so you can practice on the course that you will be visiting.

Earn Your Wings

If you have always wanted to fly a plane, you can try it on the computer first. Flying programs have become so sophisticated that even licensed pilots find them incredibly realistic. You can choose the type of plane that you will fly, from a glider to a Lear jet. Some versions of these programs have a ground school where you can learn the basics before you fly. They also offer realistic scenery. You can choose the weather conditions, time of day, and other flight parameters. You decide where you want to fly and chart your course. Landing at O'Hare Field in Chicago can be quite different than landing at the Heathrow Airport in London. Don't worry about the crashes: I am told that most people do get better with practice. One thing to watch out for is disk space. Even CD-ROM versions of flight programs can take up quite a bit of disk space. Check this out before you buy.

Your Favorite Pursuit

The computer provides a world of fun for the hobbyist. Whether your hobby is coin collecting or carpentry, there are computer programs that you can enjoy.

Let me give you a run-down on programs that are available for some of the more popular hobbies.

Cooking

The computer is a valuable resource for cooking enthusiasts. Some of the best cookbooks available have been published in computer versions. You can search these books for recipes by title, type of food or ingredient. For instance, if you have a taste for bananas, with the click of a mouse you have a list of recipes that use bananas. You can often change the number of servings for a recipe automatically. If the recipe serves 4, but you are having 10 for dinner tonight, enter the number 10 and the ingredients will be automatically updated for you. You can put all of your recipes into the computer. Some programs will give you an analysis of how much fat each recipe contains. You don't need to have your computer in the kitchen. You can print out recipes as you need them, or print them on index cards for your kitchen file.

Genealogy

Have you taken up genealogy as a pastime? The computer can be beneficial to you if you have. There are several outstanding genealogy programs that are designed to help you organize your data. They can also help you locate your ancestors through built-in databases and leads that find the proper resources for your research.

One company has a system which allows you to send in your family tree. Then you can access the database they've created from the information that everyone who owns their program has sent in. This information is not documented, but it might lead you to the missing link in your family tree. If you are doing a thorough job in your research, you can easily accumulate mounds of data. Genealogy programs allow you to access your information easily. They also give you many options for printing the tree. I wouldn't want to do any research of this type without a computer.

Travel

If travel is your hobby, use the computer to scout out new places to visit. The Internet is a rich resource. Almost every

community has a Web page on the Internet. You can choose the restaurants that you will eat in and review the menu before you leave home. If you would like to travel but don't have the time or money, you can still plot out a trip. Remember, half of the fun is in the planning— dreaming might bring your trip a little closer to reality.

Even if you don't travel around the world, you can use the computer to travel around your neighborhood. The Internet has map search sites where you can type in an address and get a map showing the exact location. You can also purchase programs called street guides or atlases that will help you find anyplace in the world. These programs can also help you plan the fastest, shortest or most scenic route for a car trip. They will suggest sites to see on the way and figure the exact mileage and cost for gasoline.

Your Creative Outlet
Drawing and Painting Programs

There is a significant difference between standard drawing and painting programs. Drawing programs use the computer's graphic abilities to create a picture in the same way that you would use colored pencils to draw a picture. A paint program duplicates brush strokes and textures in the same way that you would use a set of oil paints and paint brushes.

High-end programs, such as CorelDraw or Fractal Design Painter, maintain this clear-cut distinction. Less expensive programs have blurred the lines between drawing and painting. Some programs allow you to do both.

A drawing program allows you to create and manipulate images. In using a program of this type you will learn to create many different types of objects. You will also learn to align objects to each other, to group objects together so that you can work with them as one entity, and to use options like *send to the front* or *send to the back* to layer objects on top of one another. Drawing programs are excellent for creating line drawings and logos.

Painting programs allow you to produce art that mimics designs developed with traditional tools. You will be able to choose brushes, charcoal, watercolors or oils. Dedicated paint programs will often allow you to simulate the styles of the great artists like Seurat or Van Gogh. This is a wonderful place to get your creative juices flowing.

You will find that different graphics programs create and work with different types of graphic file formats, such as BMP, JPG, PCX and TIF. Hopefully, software developers will enable these formats to work together. In the meantime, we have to worry about changing file formats. Changing files from one format to another is called *file conversion*. In some programs you can take a file in one format and simply save it in another format. In other programs you must use import and export functions to perform the same task. If you decide to work with graphics files, you will have to educate yourself a little further about file formats.

"Skill to do. . .comes from doing."

— Ralph Waldo Emerson

Desktop Publishing

Desktop publishing is the art of creating reports, newsletters, brochures, magazines, books and other publications on a personal computer. Desktop publishing programs create a designer look to documents by combining text and graphics. You can create graphics in a drawing program or picture in a paint program, and import them into your desktop publishing document. This is a good feature to use if you want to customize your document by adding a company logo or picture. You can also use *clip art* to add pizzazz to your work. Clip art is a set of graphic images that you can copy and use in your work. Drawing programs and desktop publishing programs both come with their own clip art collections. You can also purchase clip art collections on disk or on CD-ROM to increase your choices. You can find clip art on just about any subject.

Desktop publishing programs allow you to have control over text in ways that surpass many word processing programs. Since their emphasis is on integrating text and graphics into one document, they allow you to wrap text around the graphics to create visually appealing pages. You can also have more control over the various aspects of type, such as *leading* and *tracking*. Leading is the space between lines of text, like single-space, double-space, etc. Tracking is the space between letters. If you want to have control over all of these items, you can. If you don't want to be bothered with these details, buy a program that has wizards or other helpers that will set it all up for you automatically.

Desktop publishing is not just for newspaper professionals. It is for everyone. I even suggest that teenagers and preteens get involved in using these great programs. Choose a program such as Microsoft Publisher, which is inexpensive and easy to use. Then start creating different documents. You'll be amazed at the quality of the documents that you can create with a simple program and an inexpensive color ink jet printer. You'll be surprised at the possibilities for creating newsletters, brochures, banners, signs, calendars, post cards, flyers, cards and invitations. You can even make bookmarks, bridge tallies, certificates, origami and paper airplanes.

For Movie Buffs Only

Have you ever gone to the video store and not known which movie you wanted to rent? Or are you an old movie buff? In either case, there is a type of computer program that was designed with you in mind. These programs offer movie reviews and much, much more. The program gives you background on the actors and actresses, producers and directors. It includes movie clips, still photos and music. One nice feature with most of these programs is that you can look up a movie even if you only know part of its name. You can also create lists of your favorite movies or movies that you would like to rent.

Like encyclopedias, some of these programs can be updated through the Internet. Every year, a new CD-ROM is issued with completely updated information. This is also available on a yearly subscription basis.

Photo Programs

Not too long ago, software that works with photographs was only available for professionals using high-end machines. Now these programs are available for the casual photographer as well as for the casual computer user. These easy-to-use, inexpensive photo programs can remove red eye, add special effects or combine two different photos. Built-in templates allow you to add photos to greeting cards, calendars and posters. You will find amazing special effects with these programs, as well as a ready collection of stock photos, backgrounds and frames for you to choose from. You can make everything from a calendar with family photos to a newsletter with pictures of your entire staff.

Although you can be very productive and have lots of fun with photo programs, just be sure that you have adequate computer resources—photos take up a considerable amount of disk space. Don't even think about working with photographs if your hard disk is smaller than one gigabyte. As always, with hard disk space, the more you have the better off you are.

You can use these programs with only the stock photographs that come with the program, or you can customize documents by adding your own photos. To do this you should have a scanner to scan in photos, a digital camera or other video input device. If you do not have one of these devices, you can have your pictures developed on CD-ROM. If your local photo store is not able to do this for you, there are plenty of mail-order companies that provide this service.

Also, you will probably want to print the great documents that you create. A color printer is not a necessity, however it will greatly enhance your output.

Board Games

Some of you will remember playing board games when you were a kid. It wasn't just the challenge of the game that was exciting, the camaraderie and interaction between the players made the game enjoyable. Today, 3D graphics and sound bring games such as Monopoly, Yahtzee, Clue and Scrabble to life. Some of these programs have added graphics, interactive abilities and other features. In Clue, for example, you can locate and examine the potential murder weapons, cross-examine suspects and locate the room where the murder took place. If you miss playing board games with your sister  or brother, who now lives across the country, don't worry. Many of these games can be played on the Internet. If you don't have an opponent in mind, there are Internet groups that you can join.

In Monopoly, you can ruthlessly compete against worthy adversaries on a global basis, perhaps even participate in the Monopoly World Championship each year. Remember the times when you wanted to play a game and no one else would play with you? The computer has solved that problem.

If you want to give your brain a little workout, learn to play chess, or improve your playing abilities. Chess programs are not only remarkable learning tools, they can be fun. You will be amazed by the different twists that some of the computer programs have given to this game. Animation has allowed the chess pieces to come alive—creative minds have given them many new shapes and sizes.

Fun for the Kids

Software developers have created a myriad of educational and entertaining children's programs.

Preschoolers can learn their letters, numbers, shapes and colors with Dr. Seuss, the Muppets or their favorite Sesame Street characters.

Software is often tied to the most popular current children's movie. For instance, when *Toy Story* was a smash hit at the movie theaters, there were several *Toy Story* software titles written. The release of *101 Dalmatians* spawned several programs, which featured those irresistible spotted dogs. Some of these programs are quite good; others are just riding on the coattails of a popular movie. This is one area where you should be especially careful to read software reviews and try to determine how good the program is before you buy.

Try to have the children who will use the software try it out in the store or at a friend's house. You will usually get an immediate reaction regarding their likes or dislikes. To be honest with you, I have tried several pieces of children's software that I wouldn't mind playing with. Some of these programs are out of this world!

I find that some of the most creative software available is aimed at elementary school children, geared to bringing out a child's creativity. The computer interface excels in this area. There are creative writing programs and creative drawing programs. Let your children try as many of these as possible.

Their natural talents and affinities often surface at an early age when given the opportunity to experiment. The multimedia features of children's software are usually some of the best on the market. Children today are growing up with computers; they expect the best and the software developers respect that by producing the best for them.

Educational software is often combined with multimedia features. This creates an exciting way for children to learn geography, art, music and history. Children will often find these as entertaining as adults do.

If you can get your teenagers away from the pinball and shoot-em-up games, they will also find many multimedia titles to choose from. Educational software for teens has a strong emphasis on math and science. You can find wonderful programs that teach physics, chemistry and geometry. Software can be used to prepare your teen for taking the SATs and to help him or her find the right college. Most teens also enjoy astronomy programs. If your teens are creative, have them try out the movie making programs, where they can direct an entire movie.

You and Your Computer Can Make Beautiful Music Together

When CD-ROM technology came to the computer, it allowed users to play music CDs on their computers. It also allowed software developers to use sound to enhance their programs. Sound has become an integral part of the personal computer, especially in the home market. Improvements and price reductions in soundboards have given the computer a fine voice.

By adding high quality speakers to their computer systems, computer users are now able to enjoy great sound from their personal computers.

If you are purchasing a new computer, you need sound to take advantage of the multimedia functions that are available. You can also work with the sounds that your computer can produce to create an interesting and desirable working environment. Within the operating system, you will find the basic tools that are necessary to work with and manipulate sounds. Once you have mastered these simple tools, you can purchase programs that allow you to create your own sounds, and compose and print music. These programs range in scope from beginner to advanced.

If you would like to hook up an instrument to your computer, it must be MIDI compatible. Many keyboards and guitars are compatible. Check with the manufacturer of the instrument if you are not sure. Also, you might need a special adapter. Check with your computer manufacturer. You can hook up any MIDI-compatible instrument to your computer. If you would like to learn to play the piano, or to compose music, this is a great place to begin.

Have Fun With Your Computer

Even though I am not a game lover, I do have a few things that help me remember to have fun with the computer. I have a large gray and white mouse head that sits on top of my monitor. This mouse has no body; his arms are attached to the sides of the monitor and his feet sit underneath. He is always there to remind me to lighten up when things get too stressful. Now, I know that the football-player types do not want a fluffy mouse on their computer, but they might want to buy a mouse pad with their favorite team on it. Get some floppy disks with Bugs Bunny on them or some stickers with appropriate sayings on them to put on the sides of your monitor. Keep it light and have some fun.

A Summary . . .

The personal computer has some-thing for everyone to enjoy.

- *Games*

- *Sport-Related Programs*

- *Travel*

- *Genealogy*

- *Cooking*

- *Drawing and Painting*

- *Desktop Publishing*

- *Photo Programs*

- *Music*

Check out the appendix for specific recommendations.

Communicating With the World

───◆───

Chapter 12

"Think like a wise man but communicate in the language of the people."

— *William Butler Yates*

The computer has become a means of communication for millions of people. Invented to do computations, it has quickly evolved into a communication and information tool for the world. Communicating by computer, with constant technological improvements, leads the way to our evolution into today's computer culture.

At the heart of computer communication is the modem. This allows one computer to communicate with another. Each computer must be equipped with a modem for the two computers to "talk" to each other. One modem initiates the call. When the other modem responds successfully, a connection is established, and you are said to be *on-line*. When the connection is terminated, you are *off-line*.

Modem speed is very important. Sometimes you will find that, even though you have a fast modem, it seems to connect at

a slower speed. In order for modems to communicate with each other, they must both transmit data at the same rate of speed. If you have a 28,800 Bps modem but the computer that you are connecting to has a 14,400 Bps modem, the connection will be made at the slower speed. The higher-speed modem will usually auto detect the slower modem on the other end and adjust its speed to match.

Modem Settings

The settings that modems use may seem quite complicated. You will find terms such as *parity*, *data bits*, *stop bits* and *duplex*. Better communications programs take care of the modem settings for you. I recommend that you use a good software program and not worry about these details, unless you are interested in finding out more about modem communications.

Sending and Receiving Files by Modem

Modems are used to send files across telephone lines. If you send a file to someone else, you are said to *upload* the file. If you receive a file from another computer, you *download* the file.

Transferred files use a complex method of controlling the data and checking it for errors. This is called a *file transfer protocol*. These settings are not usually a concern.

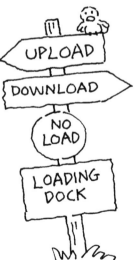

You will rarely have to make a choice of protocol. However, when dealing with some bulletin board systems you might be asked what protocol you want to use. Just remember to work your way back from the end of the alphabet. ZMODEM is usually the best protocol to use. If that doesn't work, try YMODEM or XMODEM. One of them will work most of the time. You don't need to investigate the detail unless you plan to do quite a bit of file transferring in this manner.

File Compression Revisited

File compression, as mentioned earlier, makes files smaller so they take up less space on a hard disk. It also reduces the size of the files so that they transmit more quickly over phone lines. Sometimes you will find that a file has been sent to you, or downloaded, in a compressed format. The most commonly used file compression program is named PKZIP. A file compressed with this program is also referred to as a zipped file. It will have a file name with .zip at the end. If you get such a file you need to get a copy of PKZIP, a common shareware program, to unzip the file before you can use it. You can get it from a friend or download it from the Internet or almost any bulletin board.

Bulletin Boards

A bulletin board system (BBS) is simply a large computer, or group of computers, run by some organization or

a dedicated computer operator. Most of these systems are open to the general public. Some are devoted to a certain organization or group of people with a common interest. A great variety of subject areas are covered, from a computer user's group or computer products to dating services. Bulletin boards are now dwindling in numbers with the explosion of the Internet.

Faxing From Your Computer

Many modems have fax capabilities built in, allowing you to fax documents directly from your computer. I recently faxed a 50-page document from North Carolina to Sweden. In less than two minutes, the document was on its way. If I had sent that document by traditional fax machine, I would have had to print it first, then hand feed the sheets into my old fax machine. In this instance, my computer saved me a considerable amount of time.

There is one major drawback. While it is easy to fax a document that was created on the computer, if you want to fax something else, for instance, a newspaper clipping, you would have to use a scanner to get that document into the computer so you could fax it.

If you plan to fax numerous documents with your computer, invest in a good communications program to handle your faxes for you. You can fax from the communication program itself or from the program that you are working in. For example, if you want to fax a letter that you have just written in your word processor, you can do so without leaving the word processing program. You just choose to print the document, choose your fax program as your printer and click *okay*. If you have a good program, it will prepare a cover sheet for you, fax the document automatically and file a copy for your future use.

"Who is wise? He who learns from everybody."

— Mishna

Internet

The Internet is a network of computers spanning the globe that can put a world of data at your fingertips. Investigate it if you have a computer and a modem. It's not only fun, but also a fantastic source of information.

The Department of Defense started the Internet in the late 1960s. It quickly grew to include scientists, scholars, researchers and computer profes-sionals. However only the acad-emic and scientific communities used it until recently.

In the overall scheme of things, the Internet is in its infancy, but developing rapidly. You will find some frustrating moments, but all in all, getting on the Internet is an experience that shouldn't be missed.

On-Line Services

A commercial on-line service, such as America Online, CompuServe, Prodigy and the Microsoft Network offer you a vast amount of information. They also allow you easy access to the Internet. On-line services offer you access to the World Wide Web, news groups and E-mail. They also give you a well-organized structure, top-notch reference resources, and tech-nical support if you have a problem. This can be a good place for a beginner to "get their feet wet" as most of these compa-nies offer free service for the first month.

When subscribing to an on-line service, you will pay a set subscription fee. Many of these services also charge by the hour; be careful not to stay on-line for too long or you could face a large phone bill. Make sure that the service has a tele-phone number that is local to your area. If you are in a small town or remote area, you could be facing some large long distance telephone bills if your modem must dial a long distance number to access the service. If you do live in an area that has no local access number, the service might offer you an 800 number to use. Again, check this out carefully. Even though it is a toll free number, you will often be charged on a per minute basis for use of this number.

Some on-line services have what they call *premium features* at extra charge. For example, if you access certain business *forums* on CompuServe, there will be an additional fee involved. You will be notified of this before you enter the forum. The additional cost will automatically be put on your bill.

A *forum* is a special interest group, somewhat like a virtual community, where people come together to exchange ideas and information on a certain subject. There are forums on business and computer issues, as well as hobbies, professional networks, religion, politics and just about any other subject. Forums offer a wealth of detailed information, presented in a format that is somewhat structured. Many people prefer using forums instead of the more or less unstructured information of the Internet.

Just like everything else in the fast-moving world of computers, on-line services are constantly changing with growing pains and constant restructuring. You might want to try all of them, since they all offer a free trial period.

Here is a brief synopsis of four of the major services to help you decide about where to begin:

- America Online (AOL) is the easiest service to use. It is a good place to meet people and chat about common interests.

- CompuServe is the best service for business or computer related resources. The personal computer advice and technical support is outstanding. Surcharges here can add up quickly, but are sometimes worth it, especially for in-depth business information or computer help.

- Microsoft Network is constantly changing and improving. It offers good content for most interests.

- Prodigy has long been known as the family-oriented service, but it seems to be changing that image. It has good material for kids, students and parents.

> **TIP** Always sign off an on-line service properly. Usually typing bye or clicking an icon to hang up does this. If you just turn your modem off it might take awhile for the service to realize that you are no longer on the line. You will be charged for time that you did not actually use.

Finding Your Internet Connection

You can access the Internet through an on-line service, but if you just want the Internet without any frills, you can connect directly.

If you are a student at a large University, a government worker, or work for a large corporation that provides access to the Internet, you will not have any cost involved in hooking up. However, if you are not attached to any such group, you must pay a fee to access the Internet from your home or office. While the Internet itself is free, you will be paying a fee to the company that provides you the telephone hook-up to the Internet.

Such companies are called *Internet Service Providers*. Your first step in accessing the Internet is to find a good provider in your area. The best way to do this is to ask friends, relatives and neighbors for recommendations. You can also check the yellow pages and newspaper ads for the names of providers. Here are some of the more important things to look for:

- Look for a company that has a local phone number. Long distance charges add up quickly.

- Make sure that all the services you want are included. E-mail is usually included, but not always. If you want to maintain your own Web page, ask if server space is included in your account. (It often is.)

- Avoid frustration by making sure that your Internet provider has adequate lines to handle all of their customers. You want to avoid busy signals. Again, check this out with friends and neighbors.

- Make sure that the service offers modem connections of at least 28.8 Kbps. Even if you don't own a modem that fast, you might want to buy one after you determine how much you like the Internet.

- If you are new to computers and/or the Internet, you will need an Internet provider that has good technical support. Check out the quality of the technical support service and the hours when that service is available.

- Compare prices. There is usually a set-up fee, which

varies from one company to another. Some providers offer unlimited access for a set price. Others charge by the hour.

- Many companies are offering free trials. If you do this, ask if the company will return your set-up fee if you terminate your subscription within the trial period.

The World Wide Web

The Internet has existed for many years in a non-graphical format. In the past, in order to communicate over the Internet, you used text and characters such as $ and %. These instructions to access information were UNIX-based commands. You had to know the "language" to be a part of the information exchange.

All of that changed with the advent of the *World Wide Web*. The Web is the part of the Internet that uses new methods of communication, allowing information to be presented in a graphic format. You can view pictures, colors and realistic representations of objects. It opens up the Internet to a fast-
growing world of exciting possibilities. The Web is the most user-friendly part of the Internet.

The creation of the World Wide Web's graphical structure was made possible by the introductions of *HTML* and *HTTP*. *Hypertext Markup Language* or HTML is the set of codes and instructions that creates the graphical Web documents. *Hypertext Transfer Protocol* (HTTP) defines the rules and conventions for sending and requesting information. All the computers that communicate with each other over the Web use this protocol, or set of rules.

You don't have to know anything about HTTP or HTML to use the Web. You will be using a software program that will access the text, graphics and data for you. It will act as the interface between you and the computer. This program is called a *Web Browser*.

Mosaic, one of the first Web Browsers is still used today. It was written by the National Center for Supercomputer Applications (NCSA) at the University of Illinois.

However, it has been overcome in popularity by two other browsers, Netscape's *Navigator* and Microsoft's *Internet Explorer*. One of these two programs is usually given to you when you sign up for your Internet access with an Internet service provider. America Online, CompuServe and Prodigy offer built-in browsers as part of their service.

Netscape and Microsoft are in a race to see which company can take control of the browser market. As each new version becomes available, they seem to leapfrog over each other. Netscape might be the best right now; Microsoft might be the best a month from now. Features in each program are similar. You might try both programs and see which one you like better, or just use the browser that came with your Internet connection.

Surfing the Web

The pages of information on the Web are like the pages of information in a book. In fact, each site on the Web is called a *Web page*. On the Web, instead of turning page after page, you jump from one page to another.

When you find a page that you may want to go back to, you *bookmark* that page. This is as easy as clicking on an icon marked *bookmark*, or choosing *bookmark* from a menu. The page will be added to a bookmark menu. When you want to return to a page that you have bookmarked, you simply choose that page from your list. The program will take you to that page automatically.

When you are looking at a page on the Web, you will notice that some words are underlined or printed in a different color (or both). These are called *hypertext links*. Clicking your mouse on one of these hypertext links will take you to another page. You can jump from one page to another quite easily. You can also click on the buttons marked "Back" and "Forward" to move around pages that you have already viewed. This ease of navigation, is what spawned the term "surfing the Web."

Creating a Home Page

Many groups and individuals that have their own site on the Internet are said to have a *home page*. If you would like to create your own home page, you can do so fairly easily by writing instructions in HTML with a simple software program. You might even be able to use a software program that you already own. For instance, if you have a current version of Microsoft Word, type in and format your information, as you like. Save the document in HTML format and you have instantly created a Web page.

After you create a Web page, you must publish it on the Internet for everyone to see. You can contact your Internet service provider for instructions on how to do this.

An on-line service like CompuServe provides all the necessary software and instructions for setting up a home page on the Web.

What's a URL?

Each page on the Web has it own address. A Web page address is also called a *Uniform Resource Locator*, or *URL* (pronounced "earl"). A typical URL would look like this:

http://www.nytimes.com

The first part of the address, before the colon, is the access method. Most of the time you will see *http*, which means you are accessing a web page.

The colon and the slashes are special separators that the computer understands. They are UNIX codes, used by most computers on the Internet. For those of you who are familiar with DOS, you will find that DOS uses the backslash (\) while UNIX uses the forward slash (/).

After the slashes, you will find the name of the place where the information is located. It often contains the letters www for World Wide Web.

E-Mail

Electronic mail (E-mail) is a process that uses computers to send, receive, store and forward messages. Most E-mail travels through the Internet, but many offices and on-line services have their own E-mail network.

E-mail offers reliability that rivals the traditional post office, while providing the speed and efficiency of a telephone call. When using E-mail there is no cost, except for the cost of your Internet or on-line connection. This makes using E-mail very attractive for communicating with distant friends or relatives. E-mail has quickly become the most popular use of the Internet since it is the fastest, most inexpensive and convenient way to communicate with other computer users.

E-Mail Software

When you sign up with an on-line service or an Internet service provider, you will get an E-mail account and the necessary software that you need to send and receive mail. The Internet browser that you use will probably have E-mail capabilities built into it, and this is generally a convenient way to deal with your mail. If you find that you need additional features, you can get another program later.

Most E-mail software has similar features. There is an *in-box* where your new, unopened mail is delivered. Open your mail, by clicking the mouse. That piece of mail is then displayed on your screen. After you read the mail, you can send it to the wastebasket or store it in a file for future reference. You can also reply to the mail by clicking on a *reply* icon. Compose your reply and click on the *send* icon. The program will address the reply for you automatically.

Your program will also have an *out-box* for mail that has already been sent. You can check your out-box to make sure that the message has been sent.

Mail programs have built-in address books for you to store the E-mail addresses of all the people that you correspond with. To compose E-mail, choose the correct name from your address book. The E-mail address will automatically be put into the proper place on your correspondence. This feature is a real timesaver.

Addressing E-Mail

Just as you need an address to mail a letter at the post office, you also need an address to E-mail correspondence. E-mail addresses generally look something like this:

person@place.type. The first part of the address indicates the user name of the person you are trying to reach. The user name might be a first name, last name, or combination of both. It might also be a nickname or other name that the user chose or was given when he signed up for E-mail. The @ symbol in the address is simply used to separate the user name from the rest of the address. It is a necessary part of the address. After the @ symbol you will find the name of the *domain*, which indicates the network where the user is located, followed by a period. This can be considered the place that the user's mail is received. The domain is followed by an extension that indicates the type of organization to which the network belongs.

Some common extensions are:

com for commercial business or company

edu for educational institution

gov for government agencies

int for international

mil for military

net for network organizations

org for organization (nonprofit)

You might also see foreign addresses that add a country code as the last several digits of the address, such as:

au (Australia)

ca (Canada)

fr (France)

it (Italy)

th (Thailand)

us (United States of America)

As you know, new area codes are added to accommodate growing numbers of telephone users. The same thing is already happening to Internet addresses. Many new domains are being added to support new Internet users.

One thing to remember is that you must type the E-mail

address **exactly**. If even one digit is wrong, it will be returned to you. Also, there are no spaces in Internet addresses. This is a common error that is easily correctable.

Getting Your Own Domain Name

When you get your own domain name, you are essentially getting a new numerical address. For example, the domain name *microsoft.com* is represented by the numerical address 198.105.232.4. You never need to know or use your numerical address because the computer links your domain name to your numerical address. Once you have a domain name you can keep that name forever. You can move your domain name to a new location or a new server easily and still retain the same domain name as your address.

If you have a company name or other name, you can create your own domain. Contact your Internet service provider (ISP) for easy instructions on how to do this. They will do the research to find out if the name you want is available. Or, you can research this yourself on the Internet. Then, you register the name that you want. In a few weeks your new domain name will be activated.

You will pay the company that registers the domain name a set yearly fee. You will also pay your Internet provider a fee for hosting or keeping your domain name on their file server. This fee varies greatly from one ISP to another. Be sure to check this out.

My domain name is compukiss. You can reach me at: sandy@compukiss.com

Netiquette

The Internet has spawned a new type of etiquette.

The Internet and E-mail provides a certain kind of inter-action between individuals that is unique in the world today.

There will be times when you so strongly disagree with another's opinion that you would like to respond with a posting or E-mail that shows excessive outrage or personal attack. This is so common on the Internet that they  even have a name for it. It is called *flaming.* Sometimes flame wars develop between groups of people. If you feel like flaming someone, my best advice is this: Take a deep breath, hang up your modem and think about it a little before you take action.

With the Internet, it is easy to send messages to multiple people. A new kind of junk mail, called *spamming* is the result. This is not only bothersome, but in many states it is illegal.

Some Internet providers will cancel your account if you are caught flaming or spamming.

Please remember that the E-mail you send is a reflection 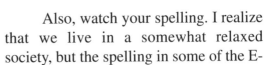 of you. Even if you are not a touch typist, try to use the proper capitalization. When I receive an E-mail from someone who does not capitalize anything, I can't help but think that this might be an indication of their inherent laziness.

Also, watch your spelling. I realize that we live in a somewhat relaxed society, but the spelling in some of the E-mail that I receive is very poor. If your E-mail software does not have a good spell checker you might want to upgrade it. You can also compose your E-mail in your word processor and spell check it there. Then you can *cut it* out of your word processor and *paste it* into your E-mail.

Remember that E-mail and postings on newsgroups can travel around the world. While researching this book, I sent an E-mail to an American company. The response came from a woman working for that company in South Africa. She didn't know the answer so she passed it on to someone else. The second response came from Australia. That party forwarded my question to someone else. The actual answer to my question came from a gentleman in Charlotte, North Carolina. Remember, you don't always know who your E-mail will reach. Not everyone on the Internet has the same customs or background. Try to be respectful of this in your correspondence.

Never assume that E-mail is confidential. Without encryption, the possibility exists that E-mail can be accessed and read by others. Your recipient can also forward it to others, as in my example above. The rule to follow is easy: Don't send anything that you wouldn't mind seeing on the evening news.

Typing in all capital letters is considered *SHOUTING*. If you need to make a stronger point, you can surround a word with *asterisks*.

Emoticoms

Since none of us enjoy typing too much, many shorthand expressions have become commonplace in E-mail and on the Internet. You will run across many acronyms. I'll give you a brief rundown here:

BTW means *by the way*

IMHO means *in my humble opinion*

EOL means *end of lecture*

RSN means *real soon now* (usually uttered in jest)

TIA means *thanks in advance*

BRB means *be right back*

LOL means *laughing out loud*

GMTA means *great minds think alike*

((((((name)))))) means *hugs to the person named*

You will also find abbreviations that show emotion. These are usually some form of a smiley face, such as:

:-) or :) smiling (tip your head to the left to see this.)

:-(or :(frowning

>:| angry

;-) winking

Since you can't hear voice inflection over E-mail, these *emoticoms*, as they are called, have become quite popular. The smiling face is often used to denote a sarcastic or joking statement. The frowning face says that the user did not like the last statement or is upset or depressed about something.

Hangup on the Internet

Computer users are signing up for Internet access in record numbers.

Even if you have an account that offers you unlimited access for a set monthly charge, it is a good practice to be as brief as possible.

You should log onto the Internet, retrieve your mail, then immediately log off. For users with an average amount of E-mail, this will probably take two minutes or less. Your mail is still available for you to read when you are off-line. If you would like to respond to your mail or write new mail, do so while you are off-line, then log on to send your mail. Many users stay on-line while they read and compose mail. If each user stays on-line while they do this, and each Internet service has hundreds or thousands of users…well, you get the idea.

Another way that you can help to keep the telephone lines free is when you use your browser.

A typical Internet session might go like this: You log on and start Netscape Navigator or Internet Explorer (your browser). You are interested in looking up a certain subject, so you hit the search button. You type in your subject and get a list of web pages that are appropriate. You go to the first page. It looks great. You bookmark it so that you can go back and read it later. You go to the second page and it looks good too. You skim the page. It has a link that seems interesting so you click it and you are now viewing your third page. Up to this point, you have been on-line for only about five minutes. You read that third page and then go back to the two previous pages; read both of them; print one of them and then log off.

You could have logged off the Internet sooner and saved on-line time. When you log off, the information that you accumulated in Navigator or Explorer stays in the computer's memory, until you close the program. So, if you had logged off the Internet after you got to the third page, you could have still read that page. You could have clicked on the "back" button and read or printed the two previous pages as well. The amount of information that stays in your computer can vary depending upon the settings in your program. You can change this setting, by changing the cache. You will find simple instructions on how to do this by looking at the *help* screen of your browser.

Newsgroups

Newsgroups are electronic discussion groups where you can meet others to discuss just about any subject. Like on-line forums, newsgroups cover a wide variety of topics, both general and specific. When you visit a newsgroup you are able to read the messages that were written by all the others who have accessed that group. If you respond to a message, everyone else will be able to read your response. *Usenet* is the place where you can find a collection of thousands of different newsgroups.

Accessing these groups is as simple as clicking on the *Newsgroups* icon in your browser and following a few instructions. Once you are in a newsgroup, you can post questions and get a variety of answers. The information that you receive here can be invaluable, or it can be grossly inaccurate. Join these groups and enjoy the company. You will probably learn some new things. Just remember that you will be dealing with many different people with a variety of different opinions.

Exciting Web Sites to Visit

Finding interesting sites to visit on the Web is quite easy. If you like to watch television, you will notice that many programs now give their Internet address at the end of the show.

When you see a show that you like, jot down the address and visit the site. It will invariably have links to other related sites.

Many major newspapers have Web sites that review other Web sites on a weekly basis. Use these as references to other sites that you might also enjoy. If you want to get information overload, find a good computer magazine. They always give a list of hot new sites, which will lead you to others. That's the beauty of the Web. Take advantage of it by traveling around as much as you please.

Discernment

When the Internet was populated by scholars and scientists the information posted there was usually fairly accurate. That is no longer true. Anyone who has a computer and Internet access can post information. The information you find on the Internet ranges from completely accurate to ridiculous hearsay.

A new set of skills is needed to sort through the information. We need to be more discerning in our acquisition of knowledge and we need to teach our children to do the same. When most of us were in grade school and high school, we accepted the subject matter without question. We didn't learn to question the source of the information until we got into college. That situation is no longer acceptable. Everyone needs to sort through the information on the Internet with a discerning eye, no matter what his or her age.

A Word of Caution

The Internet has taken on a life of its own. It has become a separate community where you can meet people, gather information and have some fun. As such, it mirrors our society in many ways, both good and bad.

Cyberspace has attracted all of the criminal types that are evident in the real world. You wouldn't walk down a busy street waving a handful of money, nor would you walk in a desolate area alone at night. In the computer world, you need to exhibit similar no-nonsense behaviors to protect yourself.

One of the pitfalls on the Internet is forgery. Unscrupulous individuals create bogus home pages and lure people to order items and, of course, to give out their credit card numbers. Make sure you are very careful about giving out your credit card number over the Internet. Some sites are secure, but many are not.

Forgery can also occur with E-mail. If someone can get

your E-mail name and password, they could send out E-mail in your name. This, of course, can be used for various scams. In the corporate environment, this can be especially dangerous. It's a good idea to use passwords and be sure to keep your passwords private.

Just as fraud is a common crime in the real world, it is also prevalent on the Internet. Electronic scams are often similar to the real world get-rich-quick schemes. You will find the on-line equivalent of chain letters and many different types of pyramid schemes. A piece of correspondence that you receive by E-mail may seem more urgent than mail received by the post office. Some of these scams carry their own unique electronic twists and turns that can make them seem very real and important. A scam is a scam is a scam. Keep away from them on the Internet just as you would in the real world.

Electronic theft is a problem not just on the Internet, but in individual situations, especially in the business world. Theft of funds, passwords and data is the most reported computer related crime. The criminal element has the edge in many situations. Security precautions have either not been instituted or have not been adequate to prevent perpetration. Over half of the attempted thefts have been completed. Many companies do not even realize that the penetration has taken place; it goes completely undetected and unreported. If you work with sensitive data, seek the help of a qualified computer consultant and initiate security precautions immediately.

If your E-mail box gets clogged with junk mail, you know the frustration it can cause. Several cases are now in the courtroom regarding the sending of unsolicited E-mail. Junk mail can be a problem that is aggravated if you give out personal information over the Internet. Sometimes you will be legitimately asked to give out information. For example, I subscribe to several services that use E-mail to distribute their information. I had to fill out a form with personal information to complete my subscription. These are great services and I am very happy with them. Sometimes it's okay to give out your E-mail address. Again, it's just like the real world. Be careful who you are dealing with and always think twice about giving out your E-mail address and personal information.

A Summary . . .

1. Your computer allows you to communicate with the world.

2. The modem is the key that creates computer communications.

3. A computer and a modem allow you to:

   • Fax information to other computers.

   • Connect to the Internet and the World Wide Web.

   • Hold discussions with other computer users through forums, newsgroups and chat lines.

Looking Ahead

◆

Chapter 13

"Your future depends on your comfort with it (the personal computer)."

Andy Grove, Intel CEO

As you go forward with the principles and lessons that you have learned from this book, you will broaden the role computers play in your life.

Now that you are more knowledgeable and confident about computers, you can better incorporate them into your daily life. Don't worry about remembering every detail you read here. Just realize that you can maneuver comfortably with computers.

Comfortably is the important word here. You will increase your comfort level only by familiarity. Try new things! The future will give you plenty of opportunity to interact with computers.

In life there is always movement, always change. Computer technology is one of the most fluid and rapidly changing things in our lives today, creating momentous improvements. As computers get better and faster, they will become a fundamental part of our lives. We have already reached the critical mass. There is no turning back.

As with most things in life, there will be both a good and bad side to many of the changes that computers bring. Many writers today look only at the bright side of the technology. I hope to give you a look at both sides of the issues, since knowing where the pitfalls are can often help you avoid them.

As we move forward into the new century, the call goes out for a computer in every home. We may not reach that goal for a while, but there will be a computer on every corner before long. As we rely more on the computer for communications, we will find more public places where computer links will be available. Computerized game parlors, restaurants, and corner computer kiosks are already commonplace.

Information is Power

When the ancient Greeks were trying to understand the universe, their main problem was lack of data. They had to gather information from the skies and their nearby environment. When they did develop a theory on something, it often took hundreds or thousands of years before that theory could be validated. Their world was very simplistic.

When computers moved to the desktop they put instant access to information at our fingertips. We not only have access to the data of thousands of years of documentation and exploration, but we have access to theories and ideas of men and women from around the world. The computer has given us the opportunity to see things not only from our own eyes, but also from the perspective of others who have different orientations and speak different languages.

Access to data is powerful. In our information age, having that access and understanding how to use it can make a big difference in our lives.

Bill Gates, Chairman and CEO of Microsoft Corp., in his book, *The Road Ahead*, paints a pretty picture of our future with computers. He glosses over the fact that computers, and the easy access to information that they create, might be a catalyst for further world conflict. The people and countries that have access to computers and available information will have a distinct advantage over people who do not.

This is already a fact of life in the business world. The pace has quickened, enabling fast and accurate responses to situations. Businesses around the globe are using the computer to give them the edge over competition.

Computer technology has filtered down to the personal-use level very quickly. The need for computer understanding is also filtering down to the indi-vidual. The gap will widen between the *have* and the *have-nots*. Those who do not have the computer skills to keep up with our fast-moving society will soon be left behind. Computer literacy will become a defining factor in the economic worth of a person.

This will also affect countries as well as individuals. Any country who doesn't keep up, will lose out.

Simplification is the Key

Earlier in this book, I talked about the computer under-going a simplification process. The glut of information that the computer brings to us also needs to be refined and simplified. As you look at the Internet, you realize that the wealth of infor-mation is overwhelming. The next step in this scenario is to bring order to the somewhat chaotic World Wide Web.

When you try to find information on the Internet, you use a search engine, such as *Yahoo, AltaVista* or *Infoseek.* These allow you to enter the subject, press the search button and find a list of pertinent web pages. You are often given a list of thousands of web sites. A recent search for the name George Washington on AltaVista produced 1,302,309 resulting pages. I could have refined the search by adding more information, or used a different search engine to produce better results. However, the fact remains that this is information overload.

As the Internet develops, there will be easier ways to locate information. Hopefully, this simplification will be one of the next improvements.

Merging Technologies

The digital revolution is here. Computer data, as you know, is in digital form. DVD (Digital Video Disc) technology is already in place for the computer. As television moves into the digital arena, the stage is set for the merging of computers and television.

Add digital telephone lines and you have a group of devices that are fluent in talking to each other. This will lead to more and more smart appliances. The technology for automating your entire house by computer is in place, waiting to be implemented. You won't have to be a computer guru to run your own home, but you will have to be familiar with computers to be a part of this scenario.

This convergence of technology will bring new ways to learn and be entertained. The exact form this evolution will take is yet to be determined. I don't believe that a television that lets you access the Internet is a powerful enough piece of equipment to be the *tool of the future*. It is just the first stab at linking the television and the computer, bringing the television into the interactive world. Other, more powerful, ways to converge these technologies will be coming shortly.

The key to this convergence, of course, will be the Internet. As the Internet grows up, it will become the center for communications. When the Internet becomes a wireless information source, it will become unbelievably powerful. It will be the medium for digital exchanges between people, computers and other devices. As these computers and devices get smaller, you will be able to travel to any location and still access your data.

Social Issues

The Internet has, no doubt, brought people together. You can easily play a game with an opponent from the other side of the globe. You can participate in a newsgroup with others from all over the world. This interaction with others can certainly help us understand others and broaden our horizons, but will it?

People tend to associate with other similar people just as "birds of a feather flock together." Because of the large numbers of participants, everyone on the Internet can find someone who shares his or her interests, background or affiliations. Groups of like-minded individuals will form. These individuals will validate each other, creating strong, unified forces. Liaisons such as this could become the impetus for the creation of much-needed change in our society. Ironically, they could also create a greater polarization of the various diverse groups in our society. We have worked for years to make our country a true melting pot where individuals are treated equally. Will the Internet of the future continue our efforts or will it create even greater problems in a more segregated world? This is a question that I cannot answer. Eventually Internet users themselves will determine this.

Identification

Right now, you have many different pieces of identification and identification numbers. You probably have a driver's license, a social security card, a bank account number, a credit card number and many other bits of information that can show who you are. Eventually, you will have only one way of identifying yourself . . . by computer. The computer will recognize

you by your face, voice, handprint, or some combination of these. The computer will know everything about you. Every purchase you make, every legal transaction you participate in and every detail of your medical history will be a part of a computerized database. This, of course, will make your everyday life easier. You will not have to carry a wallet full of identification cards. Emergency medical treatment will be quick and appropriate. Financial transactions will be fast and easy.

This scenario, however, may give you shivers up and down your spine. If you have an image of Uncle Sam looking over your shoulder at every moment, you could be right. We will experience a loss of privacy. Worse than that, our identities could be changed, damaged or even deleted by some unscrupulous computer hacker.

Science fiction of today, like Star Trek, portrays societies where working together for the betterment of man is of prime importance. Power and money are not as important as daily living. We may, in fact, actually reach that ideal state someday. In the meantime, computer technology is progressing faster than the evolution of our personalities. We will need to keep the dishonest elements in our society from ruining our future. Data encryption and other strong security measures will need to be in place before we can reach this point in computer evolution.

Virtual Reality

Virtual reality is a computer-generated environment within which people can interact. The ultimate in virtual reality would be to enter a computer-generated chamber, be surrounded by the atmosphere of your choice, and be able to interact with that environment as if it were real. For example, a computerized room could, in every way, become an excursion to the beach.

The sophisticated software necessary to develop such an environment could be written today. The powerful computers that are needed to create a detailed world such as this are on the horizon. The most difficult part would be creating the feedback necessary to trick our senses into believing the simulation.

As computer technology creeps into our daily lives, we start to realize that our senses can be more easily fooled than we might like to admit. The simple photo software that we discussed earlier can be used to manipulate photos and create a scene that never really existed. The first highly publicized event that questioned the verifiability of a photo was the O.J. Simpson trial. A photograph of O.J., wearing a pair of shoes that matched the shoe prints at the murder scene, was admitted into evidence. Experts debated whether the photo was real or had been tampered with. The photo looked real, but was it?

Most of you have seen some sort of 3-D holographic image, like a small image on the bottom of a credit card. While these are the only images that have reached general use, the work to develop holographic images has made great leaps forward. A *hologram* is like a picture or slide that was taken using laser beams. The various beams of light allow the photographed object to be reproduced with a three-dimensional effect. When the hologram is projected it takes on a life-like form. In fact, a hologram can look so real that you wouldn't be able to differentiate it from the real object. Imagine the repercussions when this technology becomes readily available and inexpensive. The fine line between reality and fiction will blur. When you say that you can't believe your eyes, you will be correct.

The Evolution of Computers to Come

The first computers were simple numerical processors. As technology improved, computer hardware and software was developed enabling the computer to perform complex computations that resulted in the various computer applications today. Up to this point, we humans have looked at computers as extensions of our minds. Programmers and developers have tried to make computers "think" in the same sequential manner as humans.

Humans can be trained in parallel thinking, but computers excel at it. Computers can do things on many different levels at one time, adapting to multiple specific environments. Computers can analyze patterns and adapt their behavior to their findings.

Computers will not just replicate human intelligence electronically; they will evolve into some new pattern of "thinking." Where this evolution in computer thinking will take us is yet to be determined, but it presents us with an exciting new frontier.

As computers get more powerful and scientists learn more about adapting them, they will become fully and completely integrated with our lives. Most of us could not imagine a world without electricity or automobiles; so it will be with computers.

218

Computers will be a part of your future. Understand and be comfortable with computers. Take an active role.

Take charge of your computer and your life!

Personal Computer Diary

---◆---

Purchasing Your Computer

Hardware Recommendations

Hardware Inventory

Software Inventory

Purchasing Your Computer

When it comes time to purchase your computer you will find a variety of computer components to choose from. Sometimes buying a computer can be difficult because the component specifications are confusing. Higher numbers are usually better, but not always. For example, a 166 MHz processor is faster than a 133 MHz processor, but a .25 DPI monitor is better than a .28 DPI monitor.

In this section I have prepared a chart of recommended hardware specifications to guide you in your selection.This chart has two columns, one marked *Good*, the other marked *Better*. You can use these to compare components and see at a glance which is better.

New and better components are constantly being introduced. Use the following information as a guideline that will help you choose your computer components both now and in the future.

Hardware Recommendations

Component	Good	Better
CPU/MHz	Pentium 166 no MMX Pentium	Pentium 200/300 MMX Pentium II
Chassis	Mini-tower	Tower
RAM	16 MB	32 MB
Cache	128 K	512 K
Hard Disk	1 GB	4 GB
Hard Drive	12ms access	10ms access
CD-ROM	12X	16X
Monitor	.28 DPI	.25 DPI
Monitor Size	15"	17"-20"
Resolution	1280x1024	1600x1200
Video Memory	1 Meg	4 Meg
Modem	33.6 Kbps No fax No voice	56 Kbps Fax Voice recognition
Sound Card	16-bit	32-bit
Speakers	4W	10-20W

Hardware Inventory

Computer

Manufacturer _____

CPU/MHz _____

Amount of RAM _____

Size of Hard Disk _____

Date of purchase _____

Serial number _____

Support phone number _____

Warranty expiration date _____

Video Board

Manufacturer _____

Amount of RAM _____

Date of purchase _____

Support phone number _____

Monitor

Manufacturer _____

Size of Monitor_____

Type of Monitor_____

Date of purchase _____

Serial number _____

Support phone number _____

Warranty expiration date _____

CD-ROM

Manufacturer _____

Speed_____

Date of purchase _____

Support phone number _____

Modem

Manufacturer _____

Speed_____

Date of purchase _____

Serial number _____

Support phone number _____

Printer

Manufacturer _____

Model number_____

Date of purchase _____

Serial number _____

Support phone number _____

Tape or Zip Drive

Manufacturer _____

Model number_____

Date of purchase _____

Serial number _____

Support phone number _____

Software Inventory

Program name _____

Version _____

Manufacturer _____

Date of purchase _____

Serial number _____

Support phone number _____

Program name _____

Version _____

Manufacturer _____

Date of purchase _____

Serial number _____

Support phone number _____

Program name _____

Version _____

Manufacturer _____

Date of purchase _____

Serial number _____

Support phone number _____

Software Inventory

Program name _____

Version _____

Manufacturer _____

Date of purchase _____

Serial number _____

Support phone number _____

Program name _____

Version _____

Manufacturer _____

Date of purchase _____

Serial number _____

Support phone number _____

Program name _____

Version _____

Manufacturer _____

Date of purchase _____

Serial number _____

Support phone number _____

Software Inventory

Program name _____

Version _____

Manufacturer _____

Date of purchase _____

Serial number _____

Support phone number _____

Program name _____

Version _____

Manufacturer _____

Date of purchase _____

Serial number _____

Support phone number _____

Program name _____

Version _____

Manufacturer _____

Date of purchase _____

Serial number _____

Support phone number _____

Recommended Software

Accounting Programs

Quick Books by Intuit: An excellent comprehensive accounting program written for people who do not necessarily have an accounting background. Automatic setup is easy to follow. Several versions are available. Quick Books Pro has some very nice extras. (Mac version available)

PeachTree Accounting by Peachtree Software: A program that covers all aspects of your business without being cumbersome. Uses double-entry accounting and is well suited for anyone with an accounting background. (Mac version available)

Calendar Programs

Calendar Creator by The Learning Company: Great program for creating any sort of calendar. Exceptional printing capabilities. Pre-formatted layouts are easy to use. Print calendars for everything from family events to office schedules. Will print over-sized wall calendars as easily as pocket-sized calendars. (Mac version available, but newest versions are PC only.)

Calendars and More by Mindscape: Great graphics let you create calendars with a young, fun look.

Checkbook Programs

Quicken by Intuit: The defacto standard. An excellent program with many features. Used by many banks for on-line banking. For simple checkbook tracking buy the standard version. If you plan on doing any involved tracking of money, buy the deluxe version. It offers some great extras. (Mac version available)

Microsoft Money: Another excellent program. Features are at same level as Quicken, but the program is not as popular.

Children's Programs

Where in the World is Carmen Sandiego? Brønderbund: Game and learning adventure combined. You travel around the world gathering clues to solve a mystery. Other titles in this series are also excellent.

KidDesk by Edmark: Give your children from age 3 and up a fun desktop of their own. Eliminates accidental access to your files.

Barbie Fashion Designer by Mattel: Design and produce unique fashions for Barbie. Print out patterns on special fabric coated-paper and assemble the entire outfit. Great creative outlet. Plan on purchasing refill kits for extra paper.

Living Books by Brønderbund: Sets of books with like titles, such as, the Dr. Seuss bundle and the Bernstein Bear bundle. Interactive books teach word recognition, vocabulary, phonics and spelling.

Clip Art

Mega Gallery by Corel: 110,000 images. Collection of vector clip art, photos, fonts, sounds and videos. Includes color clip art reference manual and file manager. (Mac compatible)

MasterClips 150,000 by IMSI: Includes color clip art as well as good black and white images, fonts, sounds, videos and a large quantity of photos. (Mac compatible)

Communications

WinFax Pro by Delrina: Makes it incredibly easy to send faxes from you computer. Automatically creates cover pages and makes faxing to several people at one time very easy. Internet and network support.

WinComm Pro by Delrina: Use for all your communication needs. Easily creates connections for bulletin boards and other digital connections.

ProComm Plus by Quarterdeck: Transfer data, collect and send information, convert faxed images to readable text.

Contact Management

Act! By Symantec: Excellent software for tracking your calls, contacts and related activities. It can help you track just about every detail of your business relationships. The program is full of excellent features. Easy to use but takes some time to investigate and use the many features. Most customizable contact manager. (Mac version available)

GoldMine by GoldMine Software Corp.: One of the best contact managers to use for workgroups.

Janna Contact Personal by Janna Systems: Good interface. Manages contacts easily. Unlimited custom fields.

Database

FileMaker Pro by Claris Corp.: One of the easiest to use and best entry-level databases. (Mac version available)

Lotus Approach by Lotus Development Corp.: Very powerful and easy to learn. Simple databases can be created easily.

Microsoft Access: Relational databases for all levels of users allows for easy management of information. Powerful features.

Easy to use, but complicated database applications require a large time investment.

Desktop Publishing and Design

Microsoft Publisher: Powerful, inexpensive and easy to use. Has everything you need for home or small office publications. Includes user-friendly Wizards for creating everything from greeting cards to business forms. No desktop publishing experience necessary.

Print Shop by Brønderbund: Easy to use. Pre-designed art, graphics and templates. Creates greeting cards, banners, certificates and more. Not as powerful or extensive as Publisher. (Mac version available)

Quark XPress: This is the program used by most newspapers and publishing houses. Features are powerful. Learning curve is fairly steep for new users. (Mac version most popular)

Adobe PageMaker: Full-fledged publishing capabilities. Easier to use than XPress, but not as popular. (Mac version available)

Educational

Math Blaster & Reading Blaster series by Davidson & Assoc.: Series of games that teach Math to ages 4 and up. (Mac version available)

Typing Tutor by Davidson: Learn to type quickly and easily.

Soft Book Maker by SoftBooks: Creates multimedia books from projects and reports. Pro version has many extra features.

Inside the SAT and ACT by Princeton Review: Includes review for both the SAT and ACT. Presents excellent strategy for test taking, study plans and an overall guide for the test takers.

Getting into College by U.S. News and World Report: A comprehensive database of colleges and universities with an excellent search tool that allows you to filter your choices.

E-mail

Eudora, Eudora Pro by Qualcomm: Eudora is a commonly used E-mail program with substantial features. Eudora Pro adds advanced filtering, spell checking and other features for heavy E-mail users. (Mac version available)

E-Mail Connection by ConnectSoft: A good standard E-mail program.

Encyclopedias

Microsoft Encarta: A true multimedia encyclopedia, great for kids and adults alike. The deluxe version comes on two CDs and holds much more information than the standard edition. (Mac version available)

Britannica CD: The granddaddy of all encyclopedias. Excellent in-depth content. Very light on multimedia functions, but provides great links for serious research. You'll pay a little more, but you'll get a lot more content. This product is not sold in retail stores. (Mac version available)

Grolier Multimedia Encyclopedia by Grolier Incorporated: Older versions were not impressive, but the newest version has increased the speed and beefed-up the content to make it a very good buy. (Mac version available)

Fun & Hobbies

Goo by Kai: Easy to use program lets you manipulate images. You can smear, smudge, move, nudge and even create real-time animations. Distort faces and other images in fun ways. Not too practical just for fun. (Mac version available)

Catz, Dogz by Virgin Interactive: Interactive pets for you desktop. Feed them, pet them, teach them tricks. Just for fun.

Hanes T-Shirt Maker: Design it, print it and iron it on. Kit includes everything you need including transfer paper, clip-art images and ready-to-use design.

After Dark by Berkeley Systems: Series of screen savers for windows and Mac that feature great animation.

Microsoft Flight Simulator: A great, very realistic flying program. You can adjust everything from your flight plan to the flying conditions. (Mac version available)

Microsoft Wine Guide: Tells you everything you need to know about wine, including information on grape-growing areas and recommendations on which foods and wines to serve together. (Mac version available)

Links by Access Software: Realistic golf game based on real courses. You can buy extra modules to expand the number of courses you can play.

Family Tree Maker by Brønderbund: Put all the details of your family together to create an extensive, organized history. Excellent printouts. Easy to use. Deluxe edition gives you records and other's family trees to help in your research.

Games

Wing Commander Series from Origin Systems: Space combat simulations with video footage of well-known actors. (Mac version available)

SimCity by Maxis: Popular simulation game that lets you create and manage a city. Terrific graphics. Very addictive. Series includes many different games. In *SimTower* you create a skyscraper. In *SimIsle* you are king of the rainforest. (Mac version available)

King's Quest from Sierra On-Line: A series of games that have become classics. On the market since 1984.

Myst from Brønderbund Software: An adventure fantasy game where you solve puzzles as you explore a beautiful series of worlds. Refreshingly done without any overt violence. (Mac version available)

Doom by id Software: Bloody combat game that has many addicted players. (Mac version available)

ChessMaster by Mindscape: Learn chess or try your luck against the computer. Classic games for replaying, in-depth teaching displays and interactive lesson plans. Good for beginner and advanced players alike. (Mac version available)

In the 1st Degree by Brønderbund: Excellent game that makes you the prosecutor trying to convict the guilty parties. Very complex game that will keep you constantly intrigued. (Mac version available)

Monopoly by Hasbro Interactive: Monopoly enters the high tech world. Graphics and animation bring an old board game to life. This game can even translate different languages and exchange foreign currency. You can find an opponent on the Internet, play against a ready-made opponent or create your own. (Mac version available)

Graphics

CorelDraw: A complete package of art and drawing tools. Features so strong that it is used by many professionals. Expect to invest some time to learn to use the program. Corel keeps old versions on the market so you can choose to get the most current features or save some money by buying an older version. Includes an impressive assortment of clip art and images. (Mac version available)

Photoshop by Adobe Systems: World standard for photo design and production for print, multimedia and Web publishing. Best image editor available. Expect a fairly high learning curve. (Mac version available)

Fractal Design Painter by Fractal Design Corp.: Turns your computer into an artist's studio. Every tool and texture imaginable, including crayons, calligraphy, oils and airbrushes. Very full-featured. You will invest some time in learning the program. (Mac version available)

Fractal Design Expression by Fractal Design Corp.: Innovative program which is a combination of a paint and draw program. (Mac version available)

Windows Draw by MicroGraphx: An inexpensive, easy to use, solid program. Not as full-featured as CorelDraw, but very good for simple tasks.

Visio from Shapeware: Simple drawing program with pre-designed stencils. Great for creation of organizational charts, room layouts, and flowcharts.

Internet Browsers

Netscape Navigator: Excellent program for surfing the web. Powerful features. Very stable. (Mac version available)

Microsoft Internet Explorer: Excellent, full-featured, powerful program. Similar to Netscape Navigator. (Mac version available)

Language Programs

Learn to Speak Series by The Learning Company: This series includes Spanish, French, German and English. You can start with no knowledge of the language and move to the intermediate level. Interactive program allows you to compare your pronunciation with that of native speakers. (works on both PC and Mac)

Berlitz Think and Talk by The Learning Company If you are taking a trip to a foreign country, this program will give you an introductory lesson in conversational Italian, French, German and Spanish. (works on both PC and Mac)

Movies & Movie Makers

Cinemania by Microsoft: Comprehensive guide to the movies. Searching is easy. Very good multimedia features. (Mac version available)

All Movie Guide by Corel: Good movie guide similar to Cinemania, but the interface is not as good. (works on both PC and Mac)

3D Movie Maker by Microsoft: This program lets you create an animated movie or watch a movie that you have already created. Very rich in features. Easy to use. You can use simple animation tools or invest a little time to investigate the more complex tools. Excellent animation is the strength of the program. Great for teens.

Hollywood and Hollywood High by Theatrix Interactive: This program allows you to create animated movies by using preset Hollywood characters and voices. Easy to use but not as animated as 3D Movie Maker. Since you can write your own dialog the program is also a great learning tool for writers.

Music

Cakewalk Home Studio by Cakewalk: A great program for recording and printing music with your computer. Experiment with and learn about music.

Optical Character Recognition

OmniPage by Caere Corp.: Easily converts paper documents and images into useful, editable text. High degree of accuracy.

Easy to use. Works well with multi-page documents. (Mac version available)

Text Bridge by Xerox: Accurate OCR which turns all your desktop documents and images into editable text. TextBridge is especially good at translating bullets and table-formatted documents. (Mac version available)

Organizational Software

PaperMaster by Documagix: This program helps you organize your files. If you have a scanner, you can also organize all your scraps of paper.

My Professional Marketing Materials by MySoftware Company: Create professional-looking brochures and sales materials. Good program to help a small business save on printing costs.

Personal Information Managers

Ecco by NetManage: Personal Information Manager that can track telephone calls, time and expenses, schedules, to do lists and much more. Very powerful and customizable. Expect a high learning curve and leave plenty of time to set up and structure your data. If you do, you will be pleased with the results.

Time & Chaos by Isbister: Manage your address book, appointments and to do list at a glance. Allows you to view all of these on the same screen. Easy to set up, easy to use. This is a shareware program available for download on the Internet.

Lotus Organizer: Easy to use. Screen looks like a big notebook with tabs for sections. Not as powerful as some. Good for a simple calendar, address book, etc.

Outlook by Microsoft: An outstanding PIM which includes calendar, contacts, tasks and a journal. It allows you to put colored notes on your desktop for reminders. Very good

Internet integration. Outlook is a part of some Microsoft Office Suites.

Day-Timer Organizer by Day-Timers, Inc.: The Deluxe program offers all the usual calendar and to do lists plus famous quotes, a new word each day and other tips. Best program for printing calendars.

InfoSelect by Micro Logic Software: Unstructured PIM. You enter information in any place and any manner. Excellent search engine allows you to retrieve that information very easily. Great for those of you who tend to keep bits of information written on scraps of paper.

SideKick by Starfish Software: Flexible and easy to learn. Includes calendar, to-do mail merge and contact management.

Photo Programs

Microsoft Picture It: Excellent program for manipulating photos and creating calendars, cards or collages of your pictures. Backgrounds and borders are outstanding. Simple to use.

Adobe Photo Deluxe: Easy to use interface lets you add great special effects and correct mistakes easily. Comparable to Picture It. (Mac version available)

Presentation Programs

Freelance Graphics by Lotus Development Corp.: Professional strength presentation graphic program. Easy to use.

Microsoft PowerPoint: The most popular presentation program. Easy to use. (Mac version available)

Reference Books

Microsoft Bookshelf: A compilation of reference books including a dictionary, thesaurus, atlas, almanac and book of quotations. A very good interface makes it easy to use. The interface improves each year. Buy the latest version for the best features. (Mac version available.)

The Way Things Work 2.0 DK Multimedia: Version 1 was a little lacking, but version 2 is outstanding. Searches are easy. Web links give you even more information on the subject of your choice. Good choice for children and teens. (Mac version available)

Mayo Clinic Family Health Book by IVI Publishing: Basic medical information backed up with very good multi-media examples.

A.D.A.M. series by A.D.A.M. Sotfware, Inc.: A series of programs on human anatomy. Detailed graphics explain how the body works. (Mac version available)

Spreadsheets

Excel Microsoft: Loaded with features. Powerful analysis tools. Every version gets easier to use. Excel is the industry standard in spreadsheets. (Mac version available)

123 by Lotus Development Corp.: A good strong spreadsheet program with templates to help you prepare everyday forms.

QuattroPro by Novell: Another good spreadsheet with excellent features.

Suites

ClarisWorks by Claris: An excellent collection of programs. Includes word processing, spreadsheet, business graphics and database. It is a light version of the office suites. Good program but does not have a large base of users. If you need to share documents stick with Microsoft Office. (Mac version available)

Microsoft Office: Includes Word and Excel, the best-selling word processing and spreadsheet programs as well as the PowerPoint presentation program and a PIM. Earlier version came with Schedule, an almost unusable PIM. Newer versions come with Outlook, an excellent organizer. Professional versions add Access, an excellent database. (Mac version available)

Microsoft Small Business Edition: Microsoft has customized their suite program by offering several excellent combinations of their programs. This edition includes Word, Excel, Publisher, Financial Manager, Auto Map and Internet Explorer. Excellent value for home as well as small business.

Perfect Office by Novell: Includes WordPerfect, Quattro Pro, Corel Presentations and the Paradox database. Some versions also include Corel Flow which as a large clip art collection; Sidekick, a personal information manager; Dashboard, a mediocre program designed to maximize personal productivity; Envoy, an electronic publisher; and Netscape Navigator.

Smartsuite by Lotus Development Corp.: Includes Word Pro, Lotus Organizer, Freelance Graphics presentation software, Lotus Approach database and the 1-2-3 spreadsheet. Also includes ScreenCam, a program which can be used to create and distribute on-screen movies.

Quicken Financial Suite: Includes Quicken Deluxe, Financial Planner and Family Lawyer. A very useful package.

Tax Programs

TurboTax by Intuit: Plain English interviews help you fill out your taxes easily. Easily the best business-tax software. (MacInTax is the Mac version)

Telephone Directories

PhoneDisc Powerfinder by Digital Directory Assistance:

Comprehensive search capabilities with PowerFinder utility. Over 114 million listings. Can be purchased in the configuration of your choosing: home, business or combination.

Select Phone by ProCD: Similar in features to PhoneDisc, but can be purchased in different configurations. (Mac version available)

Travel

AutoMap by Microsoft: A very good program for helping you with your travel plans. Calculates the quickest, fastest and/or most scenic routes for car trips. It can even determine your cost for gasoline.

AAA Map'n'Go by DeLorme Mapping: Excellent for planning trips.

TripMaker by Rand McNally: Gives you not only detailed routing and information but links to Internet for road construction and weather information. Tailors travel information to your preferences, including camping.

Uninstallers

Cleansweep by Quarterdeck: Performs admirably in getting rid of unwanted files and programs.

UnInstaller 4 by MicroHelp: Quickly and easily removes unwanted programs and remnants of programs.

Utility Programs

PCAnywhere by Symantec: Fast and easy connection lets you access a PC remotely. Allows you to access applications and information on one PC by accessing from another PC.

Microsoft Plus! Pack: Extra utilities for Windows 95. Includes more advanced file compression programs, easy scheduling of disk maintenance, and desktop themes which include a variety of wallpapers, screen saver and cute icons.

Norton Utilities Symantec Best all inclusive program. Provides good system monitoring. Has an excellent rescue and repair disk, very good diagnostic tests, and provides for recovery of erased or corrupt files. Newer versions have additional features, like automatic updates of the program from the Internet. (Mac version available)

PKZIP, PKUNZIP by PKWARE These are shareware DOS utility programs that work with Windows to compress and decompress files.

LapLink by Traveling Software An excellent remote access program. Stay connected to your home or office computer while on the road.

Stuffit by Aladdin Systems: Excellent file compression program for Macintosh computers.

Virus Protection

Norton AntiVirus by Symantec: Complete virus protection. Works automatically in the background. Easy installation and use.

VirusScan by McAfee: On the same level with Norton AntiVirus. Has basically the same features and similar degree of accuracy in detecting viruses.

Web Publishing

Microsoft FrontPage: Lets you create a home page without learning HTML but powerful enough for serious, HTML-knowledgeable creators.

Claris Home Page: Design and develop Web pages with multi-media, links and interactive elements without learning HTML. (Mac version available)

Word-Processing Programs

Microsoft Word: The defacto standard. Excellent features. Very good interface. Easy to use yet very powerful.

WordPerfect by Novell: Was, at one time, the most popular word processor, but has been overtaken by Microsoft Word. New graphical versions have solid features and good interface.

Word Pro by Lotus Development Corp.: Good interface. Great work group capabilities allow several people to collaborate on the same document keeping track of document changes and work group capabilities allow several people to collaborate on the same document keeping track of document changes and versions.

Resource Guide

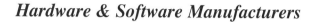

Hardware & Software Manufacturers

3Com Corp.
5400 Bay Front Plaza
PO Box 58145
Santa Clara, CA 95052-8145
800-NET-3COM
408-764-5000
http://www.3com.com

Acer America
2641 Orchard Pkwy.
San Jose, CA 95134
800-733-2237
408-432-6200
http://www.acer.com/aac/

Access Software
4750 Wiley Postway
Bldg. #1, Suite 200
Salt Lake City, UT 84116
800-800-4880
http://www.accesssoftware.com

A.D.A.M. Software, Inc.
1600 River Edge Pkwy.
Suite 800
Atlanta, GA 30328
800-755-ADAM
http://www.adam.com

Adaptec
691 S. Milpitas Blvd.
Milpitas, CA 95035
800-959-7274
408-945-8600
http://www.adaptec.com

Adobe
345 Park Ave.
San Jose, CA 95110
800-833-6687
408-536-6000
http://www.adobe.com

ALR
9401 Jeronimo
Irvine, CA 92618
800-444-4ALR
714-581-6770
http://www.alr.com

American Business Inf.
5711 S. 86th Circle
PO Box 27347
Omaha. NE 68127
800-284-8353
http://www.dda-inc.com

American Power Conversion
PO Box 278
132 Fairgrounds Rd.
West Kingston, RI 02892
800-800-4APC
401-789-5735
http://www.apcc.com

AOL Corp. Office
America Online, Inc.
8619 Westwood Center Drive
Vienna, VA 22182
800-227-6364
888-265-8009
703-448-8700
http://www.aol.com

Apple Computer
2200 Lawson Lane
Santa Clara, CA 95054
800-277-5356
http://www.uss.org

AST Research
16215 Alton Pkwy.
Irvine, CA 92618
800-876-4278
714-727-4141
http://www.ast.com

ATI Technology
33 Commerce Valley Dr. East
Thorn Hill, Ontario,
CANADA L3T7N6
905-882-2600
http://www.atitech.com

Austin Direct
10300 Metric Boulevard
Austin, TX 78758
800-752-1577
512-339-3500h
http://www.goaustin.com

Berkeley Systems
2095 Rose Street
Berkeley, CA 94709
510-549-2300
http://www.berksys.com

Britannica Direct
PO Box 22393
Denver, CO 80222
800-747-8503
http://www.eb.com

Brønderbund Software
PO Box 6125
Novoto, CA 94948-6125
800-521-6263
415-382-4400
http://www.broderbund.com

Brother International Corp.
200 Cottontail Ln.
Somerset, NJ 08875-6714
800-284-4357
908-356-8880
http://www.brother.com

Caere Corp.
PO Box 2450
Buffalo, NY 14240
800-535-7226
408-395-7000
http://www.caere.com

Cake Walk
PO Box 760
Watertown, MA 02272
800-234-1171
http://www.cakewalk.com

Canon Computer Systems
2995 Redhill Ave.
PO Box 2734
Costa Mesa, CA 92626
800-848-4123
714-438-3000
http://www.ccsi.cannon.com

Casio Inc.
570 Mt. Pleasant Avenue
Dover, NJ 07801
800-327-1266
201-361-5400
http://www.casio.com

Cheyenne Software, Inc.
3 Expressway Plaza
Roslyn Heights, NY 11577
800-243-9462
516-465-4000
http://www.cheyenne.com

Citizen America Corp.
2450 Broadway #600
Santa Monica, CA 90404
800-477-4683
310-453-0614
http://www.citizen/america.com

Claris Corp.
5201 Patrick Henry Drive
Santa Clara, CA 95054
800-325-2747
408-727-8227
http://www.claris.com

Colorado Memory Systems
800 S. Taft Ave.
Loveland, CO 80537
800-845-7905
303-669-8000
970-635-1500 (Support)
http://www.
hp.com/go/storage_support

Compaq Computer Corp.
20555 SH 249
Houston, TX 77070
800-345-1518
713-370-0670
http://www.compaq.com

CompuServe
5000 Arlington Center Blvd.
PO Box 20212
Columbus, OH 43220
800-848-8990
www.compuserve.com

Connectix Corp.
2655 Campus Dr.
San Mateo, CA 94403
800-950-5858
415-571-5100
http://www.connectix.com

Connectsoft
11130 NE 33rd Place
Suite 250
Bellevue, WA 98004
800-889-3499
http://www.connectsoft.com

Corel Corp.
1600 Carling Ave.
Ottawa, Ontario
Canada Kl Z 8R7
800-772-6735 (US)
800-394-3729 (Canada)
613-728-8200
http://www.corel.com

CoStar Corp.
599 W. Putnam Ave.
Greenwich, CT 06830-6092
800-426-7827
203-661-9700
http://www.costar.com

Creative Labs
1901 McCarthy Blvd.
Milpitas, CA 95035
800-998-5227
408-428-6600
http://www.creativelabs.com

Curtis Computer Products
2210 2nd Ave.
Muscatine, IA 52761
800-272-2366

Cyrix Corp.
2703 N. Central Expwy.
Richardson, TX 75080
800-462-9749
214-968-8387
http://www.cyrix.com

Davidson & Assoc.
19840 Pioneer Ave
Torence, CA 90503
800-545-7677
310-793-0600
http://www.davd.com

Day-Timers, Inc.
One Day-Timer Plaza
Allentown, PA 18195-1551
800-225-5005
http://www.daytimer.com

Dell Computer Corp.
1 Dellway
Round Rock, TX 78682
800-879-3355
512-338-4400
http://www.dell.com

DeLorme Mapping
PO Box 298
Freeport, ME 04032
800-452-5931
207-865-1234
http://www.delorme.com

Diamond Multimedia Sys.
2880 Junction Ave.
San Jose, CA 95134
800-468-5846
408-325-7100 (tech. support)
http://www.diamondmm.com

Digital Equipment Corp.
111 Powdermill
Maynard, MA 01754
800-722-9332
508-493-5111
http://www.windows.digital.com

DK Publishing
95 Madison Ave.
New York, NY 10016
888-342-5357
212-213-4800
http://www.dk.com

DocuMagix
2880 Zanker Rd.
Suite 204
San Jose, CA 95134-2122
800-362-8624
http://www.documagix.com

DTK Computer
770 Epperson Drive
City of Industry, CA 91748
800-289-2385
818-810-8880
http://www.dtk.com

Eastman Kodak Co.
343 State St.
Rochester, NY 14650
800-235-6325
716-724-4000
http://www.kodak.com

Edmark
6727 185 Ave. NE
Redmond, WA 98052
206-556-8400
206-556-8480 (tech. support)
http://www.edmark.com

Epson America, Inc.
20770 Madrona Ave.
Torrance, CA 90503
800-463-7766
310-782-0770
http://www.epson.com

Everex Systems
5020 Brandin Ct.
Fremont, CA 94538
800-821-0806
510-498-1111
http://www.everex.com

Fractal Design Corp.
PO Box 66959
Scotts Valley, CA 95067
800-846-0111
408-430-4000
http://www.fractal.com

Fujitsu PC Corporation
598 Gibralter Dr.
Milpitas, CA 95035
888-4-ON-THE-GO
http://www.fujitsu-pc.com

Gateway 2000
PO Box 2000
610 Gateway Dr.
North Sioux City, SD 57049
800-846-2000
605-232-2000
http://www.gwzk.com

Goldmine Software Corp.
17383 Sunset Blvd.
Suite 301
Pacific Palisades, CA 90272
310-454-6800
http://www.goldmine.sw.com

GoldStar LG Electronics, Inc.
1000 Sylvan Ave.
Englewood Cliffs, NJ 07632
201-816-2000
http://www.goldstar.co.kr..

Grolier Incorporated
Sherman Turnpike
Danbury, CT 06816
800-955-9877
203-797-3500
http://www.grolier.com

Hercules Computer Tech.
3839 Spinnaker Ct.
Fremont, CA 94538
800-532-0600
510-623-6030
http://www.hercules.com

Hewlett-Packard
3000 Hanover St.
Palo Alto, CA 94304
800-752-0900
415-857-1501
http://www.hp.com

Hitachi Home Electronics
3890 Steve Renolds Blvd.
Norcross, GA 30093
800-241-6558
770-279-5600
http://www.hitachi.com

IBM Corp.
Old Orchard Rd.
Armonk, NY 10504
800-426-3333
914-765-1900
http://www.ibm.com

IBM PC Direct
3039 Cornwallis Road
Building 203, Dept. WMD
RTP, NC 27709
800-426-2968
800-426-3333
http://www.ibm.com

id Software
18601 LBT Freeway
Suite 615
Mesquite, TX 75150
800-434-2637
972-613-3589
http://www.idsoftware.com

IMSI
1938 4th St.
San Rafael, CA 94901
800-833-8082
415-454-7101
http://www.imsisoft.com

Insight
6820 S Harl Ave
Tempe, AZ 85283
800-729-0770
602-902-1000
http://www.insight.com

Intuit Inc.
PO Box 7850
Mountain View, CA 94039
800-446-8848
415-944-6000
http://www.intuit.com

Integral Peripherals
5775 Flatiron Pkwy. Ste. 100
Boulder, CO 80301-5730
800-333-8009
303-449-8009
http://www.integral.com

Intel Corp.
1900 Prairie City Rd.
Folsom, CA 95630
800-628-8686
916-356-8080
http://www.intel.com

Iomega Corp.
1821 W Iomega
Roy, UT 84067
800-697-8833
801-778-1000
http://www.iomega.com

Isbister
1111 Belt Line road, Ste. 204
Garland, TX 75040
214-495-6724
http://www.isbister.com

IVI Publishing
7500 Flying Cloud Dr.
Eden Prairie, MN 55344
800-952-4773
612-996-6000
http://www.ivi.com

Janna Systems
308 Yonge Street
Suite 6060
Toronto, Ontario M4N3N1
800-268-6107
408-356-6647
http://www.janna.com

Kai (Kuck & Associates)
1906 Fox Drive
Champaign, IL 61820-7345
217-356-2288
http://www.kai.com

Kensington Microware Ltd.
2855 Campus Dr. #300
San Mateo, CA 94403
800-535-4242
415-572-2700
http://www.kensington.com

Key Tronic Corp.
PO Box 14687
Spokane, WA 99214
800-262-6006
509-928-8000
http://www.keytronic.com

Kingston Technology Corp.
17600 Newhope St.
Fountain Valley, CA 92708
800-337-3807
714-435-2600
http://www.kingston.com

Leading Edge Products
14 Brent Dr.
Hudson, MA 01749
508-562-3322
http://www.primenet.com

Learning Company, The
One Athenaeum
Cambridge, MA 02142
800-323-8088
http://www.learningco.com

Lexmark Int'l, Inc.
740 New Circle Rd. NW
Lexington, KY 40550
800-438-2468
606-232-2000
http://www.lexmark.com

Logitech
6505 Kaiser Dr.
Fremont, CA 94555
800-231-7717
510-795-8500
http://www.logitech.com

Lotus Development Corp.
55 Cambridge Pkwy.
Cambridge, MA 02142
800-343-5414
617-577-8500
http://www.lotus.com

Matrox Graphics Inc.
1025 St. Regis Blvd.
Dorval, Quebec
Canada H9P 2T4
514-969-6320
http://www.matrox.com

Mattel Media
333 Continental Blvd
El Segundo, CA 90245-5012
888-MATTEL9
310-252-2000
http://www.mattelmedia.com

Maxis
2121 N. California
Walnut Creek CA 94596
800-33-MAXIS
510-933-5630
http://www.maxis.com

Maxtor Corp.
510 Cottonwood Dr.
Millpitas, CA 95035
408-432-1700
http://www.maxtor.com

McAfee Associates
2710 Walsh Ave. #200
Santa Clara, CA 95051-0963
408-988-3832
http://www.mcafee.com

MicroGrafx
800-733-3729
214-234-1769
http://www.micrografx.com

MicroHelp Inc.
Marietta, GA
800-922-3383
770-516-0899
http://www.microhelp.comg

Micro Logic Corporation
89 Levning St.
South Hackensack, NJ 07606
800-342-5930
201-342-6518
http://www.miclog.com

Micron Electronics, Inc.
900 E. Karcher Rd.
Nampa, ID 83687
800-223-6571
800-438-3343
208-893-3434
http://www.micronpc.com

Micronics Computers, Inc.
45365 Northport Loop West
Fremont, CA 94538
800-577-0977
510-683-0300
http://www.micronics.com

Microsoft Corp.
One Microsoft Way
Redmond, WA 98052-6399
800-426-9400
206-882-8080
http://www.microsoft.com

Microsoft Network
One Microsoft Way
Redmond, WA 98052-6399
ATTN: MSN
800-386-5550
206-882-8080
http://www.microsoft.com

Microtek Labs
3715 Doolittle Dr.
Redondo Beach, CA 90278
800-654-4160
310-297-5000
http://www.mteklab.com

Mindscape
88 Rowland Way
Novato, CA 94945
800-866-5967
415-897-9900
415-8985157 (tech.support)
http://www.mindscape.com

Mitsubishi Electronics
5665 Plaza Dr.
Cypress, CA 90630
800-843-2515
714-220-2500

MySoftware
1259 El Camino
Suite 168
Menlo Park, CA 94025
800-325-3508
415-473-3600
http://www.mysoftware.com

Mustek
1702 McGraw Ave.
Irvine, CA 92718
800-468-7835
714-250-8855
714-247-1300 (tech. support)
http://www.mustek.com

NEC Technologies, Inc.
1250 Arlington Heights Dr.
Suite 500
Itasca, IL 60143
800-632-4636
630-775-7900
http://www.nec.com

NetManage
10725 North De Anza Blvd.
Cupertino, CA 95014
408-973-7171
http://www.netmanage.com

Netscape Communications
501 Middlefield Rd.
Mountain View, CA 94043
800-NETSITE
415-254-1900
http://www.netscape.com

Northgate Computers
10025 Valley View Rd. #110
Eden Prairie, MN 55344
800-526-2446
612-947-4600

Novell
122 E. 1700
Provo, Utah 84606
800-638-9273
801-429-7000
http://www.novell.com

Number Nine
Visual Technology Corp.
18 Hartwell Ave.
Lexington, MA 02173
800-438-6463
617-674-0009
http://www.nine.com

Okidata
532 Fellowship Rd.
Mount Laurel, NJ 08054
800-654-3282
609-235-2600
http://www.okidata.com

Electronic Arts Direct
Origin Systems Distributor
5918 W. Courtyard Dr.
Austin, TX 78730
800-245-4525
512-335-5200
http://www.ea.com

Packard Bell Electronics
1 Packard Bell Way
Sacramento, CA 95828
800-733-5858
916-388-0101
http://www.packardbell.com

Panasonic
2 Panasonic Way
Secaucus, NJ 07094
800-726-2797
201-348-7000
http://www.panasonic.com

Peachtree Software
PO Box 6150
Norcross, GA 30091
800-247-3224
770-724-4000
http://www.peachtree.com

Philips Consumer Electronics
One Philips Drive
PO Box 14810
Knoxville, TN 37914
800-835-3506
423-512-4316
http://www.philipsmagnavox.com

Pioneer New Media Tech-
nologies
2265 E. 220th St.
Long Beach, CA 90810
800-872-4159
310-952-2111
http://www.pioneer.com

PKWare
9025 N. Deerwood Dr.
Brown Deer, WI 53223
414-354-8699
http://www.pkware.com

Plextor
4255 Burton Dr.
Santa Clara, CA 95054
800-886-3935
408-980-1838
http://www.plextor.com

Princeton Graphic Systems
2801 S. Yale St.
Santa Anna, CA 92704
800-747-6249
714-751-2008
http://www.prgr.com

Princeton Review
2315 Broadway
New York, NY 10024
800-566-7737
212-874-8282
http://www.review.com

ProCD
222 Rosewood
Danvers, MA 01923
800-224-4732
508-750-0055
http://www.procd.com

Procom Technology
2181 Dupont Dr.
Irvine, CA 92612
800-800-8600
714-852-1000
http://www.procom.com

Prodigy
PO Box 8667
Gray, TN 37615
800-PRODIGY
800-213-0992
http://www.prodigy.com

Qualcomm Inc.
6455 Lusk Blvd.
San Diego, CA 92121-2779
800-238-3672
http://www.eudora.com

Quantex
400B Pierce Street
Somerset, NJ 08873
800-896-4898
http://www.quantex.com

Quantum Corp.
500 McCarthy Blvd.
Milpitas, CA 95035
800-624-5545
408-894-4000
http://www.quantum.com

QMS, Inc.
I Magnum Pass
Mobile, AL 36618
800-523-2696
334-633-4300
http://www.qms.com

Quark, Inc.
1800 Grant St.
Denver, CO 80203
800-788-7830
303-894-8888
http://www.quark.com

Quarterdeck Corp.
13160 Mindanao Way
Marina Del Rey, CA 90292
800-354-3222
573-875-0932 (tech. support)
http://www.quarterdeck.com

Rand McNally
8255 N. Central Pkwy.
Skokie, IL 60076
800-333-0136
847-329-8100
http://www.randmcnally.com

Relisys
320 S. Milpitas Blvd.
Milpitas, CA 95035
408-945-9000
http://www.relisys.com

Samsung Electronics America
105 Challenger Rd.
Ridgefield Park, NJ 07660
800-726-7864
201-229-4000
http://www.samsung.com

Seagate Technology
PO Box 66360
Scotts Valley, CA 95067
408-438-6550
http://www.seagate.com

Seikosha America, Inc.
111 Canfield Ave., A-15
Randolph, NJ 07869
800-825-5349
201-252-1040
http://www.seikoshaav.com

Seiko Instruments USA
1130 Ringwood Ct.
San Jose, CA 95131
800-553-5312
408-922-5800
http://www.cgg.seiko.com

Shapeware Visio Corp.
520 Pike St., Suite 1800
Seattle, WA 98101-4001
800-446-3335
206-521-4500
http://www.visio.com

Sharp Electronics Corp.
Sharp Plaza
Mahwah, NJ 07430
800-237-4277
201-529-8200
http://www.sharp-usa.com

Sierra On-Line
3380 146th Place SE
Suite 300
Bellview, WA 98007
800-326-6654
206-649-9800
http://www.sierra.com

Sony Electronics
One Sony Drive
Park Ridge, NJ 07656
800-222-7669
201-930-1000
http://www.sony.com

Starfish Software
1700 Green Hills Road
Scotts Valley, CA 95066
800-765-7839
888-STARFISH (order)
408-461-5800
http://www.starfish.com

Star Micronics America
70 Ethel Rd. W.
Piscataway, NJ 08854
800-782-7636
908-572-5550
http://www.starmicronics.com

STB Systems, Inc.
1651 N. Glenville #210
Richardson, TX 75081
800-234-4334
972-234-8750
http://www.stb.com

Symantec Corp.
175 W. Broadway
Eugene, OR 97401
800-441-7234
541-334-6054
http://www.symantec.com

SyQuest Technology, Inc,
47071 Bayside Pkwy.
Fremont,, CA 94538
800-245-2278
510-226-4000
http://www.syquest.com

Tandy Corp./Radio Shack
1800 One Tandy Center
Ft. Worth, TX 76102
800-843-7422
817-390-3011
http://www.tandy.com
http://www.radioshack.com

Tektronix, Inc.
PO Box 1000
Wilsonville, OR 97070
800-835-6100
503-682-7377
http://www.tek.com

Texas Instruments
13510 N. Central Expwy.
Dallas, TX 75243
800-527-3500
214-995-2011
http://www.ti.com

Theatrix Interactive
1250 45th St.
Emeryville, CA 94608
800-955-TRIX
510-658-2800
http://www.theatrix.com

Toshiba America
    Information Systems
9740 Irvine Blvd.
Irvine, CA 92618
800-999-4273
714-583-3000
http://www.toshiba.com

Traveling Software
18702 Northcreek Pkwy.
Bothwell, WA 98011-8026
800-343-8080
206-483-8088
http://www.travsoft.com

Tripp Lite
500 N. Orleans
Chicago, IL 60610-4188
312-329-1391
http://www.tripplite.com

Tri-Star Computer Corp.
2424 W. 14th St.
Tempe, AZ 85281
800-800-7668
602-731-4926
http://www.tri-cad.com

Twinhead Corp.
1537 Centre Pointe Dr.
Milpitas, CA 95035
800-995-8946
408-945-0808
http://www.twinhead.com

UMAX Technologies
3561 Gateway Blvd.
Fremont, CA 94538
800-562-0311
510-651-8883
http://www.umax.com

US Robotics
8100 N. McCormick 60076
800-DIAL USR
847-982-5010
http://www.usr.com

ViewSonic Corp.
20480 Business Pkwy.
Walnut, CA 91789
800-888-8583
909-869-7976
http://www.viewsonic.com

Virgin Interactive
18061 Fitch Ave.
Irvine, CA 92614
800-874-4607
714-833-8710
http://www.vie.com

Visioneer
34800 Campus Dr.
Freemont, CA 94555
800-787-7007
http://www.visioneer.com

Wacom Technology Corp.
501 S.E. Columbia Shores
Blvd. #300
Vancouver, WA 98661
800-922-6613
206-750-8882
http://www.wacom.com

Western Digital
8105 Irvine Center Dr.
Irvine, CA 92718
800-832-4778
714-932-4900
http://www.wdc.com

Wyse Technology
3471 N. First St.
San Jose, CA 95134
800-438-9973
408-473-1200 (not verified)
http://www.wyse.com

Xerox
Office Document Systems
800 Long Ridge Rd.
Stamford, CT 06904
800-832-6979
203-968-3000
http://www.xerox.com

Zenith Data Systems
510 Lakelook Rd.
500 Corporate Center
DeerField, IL 60015
847-236-4800
http://www.zds.com

Other Valuable Resources

1-800-BATTERIES can supply batteries for just about any portable computer and other equipment as well. Knowledgeable employees and quick service.

Multicomp 800-541-4351 LabelOnce erasable labels come with a special pen and eraser.

Paper Direct 800-272-7377 http://www.paperdirect.com Excellent source of paper products. A variety of specially designed papers for brochures, business cards, and letterhead are available.

Queblo/Paper Showcase 800-523-9080 Two lines of colorful specialty paper products.

Connected Online Backup 800-647-3078 http://www.connected.com Provides remote backup for your data.

PC Magazine 800-289-0429 http://www.pcmag.com A bi-monthly computer magazine which does many computer product reviews.

PC World 800-234-3498 http://www.pcworld.com A monthly magazine which does many computer product reviews.

Kodak 800-235-6325 or 716-726-7260 http://www.kodak.com A photo CD service lets you take pictures with regular film and have them put on a disk or CD-ROM.

Seattle Filmworks 800-filmworks http://www.filmworks.com Another good service that will put your pictures on disk or CD-Rom.

Mail-Order Hardware & Software

PC   Connection   or   Mac   Connection   800-800-0005
http://www.pcconnection.com

MicroWarehouse 800-285-7080 http://www.warehouse.com

PC Zone 800-258-8088 http://www.pczone.com

CDW 800-606-4239 http://www.cdw.com

Glossary

Active-matrix: Flat-screen liquid crystal display (LCD) in which each of the screen's pixels is controlled by its own transistor. This provides sharper contrast than passive LCD displays.

Alpha Testing: In-house testing of a software product.

Anti-virus Program: A program that searches for viruses and removes any virus that it finds.

Application: Software designed for a certain use, such as word processing. Also called a program.

Backup: (v) The process of copying important files and information from the PC's hard disk to another medium, such as floppy disks or tape. (n) a disk used to store files.

Bay: Section of the computer case where equipment like floppy disk drives and CD-ROM drives can be installed.

Beta Testing: The testing done by a software developer that includes use and reviews by outside individuals.

Bi-directional Cable: A cable that allows information to flow in both directions. Used with many newer printers.

Binary System: A numbering system based on two numbers, zero and one.

BIOS (Basic Input/Output System): A set of routines stored in the computer's read-only memory that gives the computer instructions for basic operating routines.

Bit (Binary Digit): The smallest piece of information that is recognized by a computer. It represents a 1 or a 0 in the binary numbering system.

Bookmark: To mark a document or a specific place in a document for future reference.

Boot: Derived from "boot strap. " To start or restart a computer. A cold boot means to start the computer by turning the power switch on. A warm boot is resetting a computer that is already on.

Boot Disk: (see Startup Disk)

Bps (Bits per second): The standard measure of data transmission speeds.

Browser: A software program that lets you access and navigate the Internet with a graphical interface.

Bug: A mistake in a computer program or system that causes a malfunction or erroneous result.

Bulletin Board System (BBS): A computer system that allows users to post messages and correspond with other users.

Bundled Software: Software programs that are included with the purchase of a computer or piece of hardware.

Bus: The channel or path that the computer uses to transfer data. It is the main avenue for all data that moves in and out of the computer.

Byte: Eight bits of binary information is a byte, which can represent one letter in the alphabet.

Cache: A small amount of computer memory that holds most recently used data.

Carpal Tunnel Syndrome: A form of stress injury that produces numbness or burning in the fingers, hands and/or wrists.

CD-E (Compact Disc-erasable) also called CompactDisc-RW (CD-rewritable): A compact disc that can be read, written on, erased and reused. CD-E drives can play CD-ROMs and CD-Rs as well.

CD-R (Compact Disc-Recordable): A compact disc that can be written on, but cannot be erased or reused. CD-R drives can play CD-ROMs.

CD-ROM (Compact Disc - Read Only Memory): A hard plastic disc that holds about 650 megabytes of computer data. This disc cannot be written on.

CTD (Cumulative Trauma Disorders): Physical disorders that are caused by stress on certain areas of the body.

Cell: A single location in a spreadsheet grid.

Checkbook Program: A program that helps you to balance your checkbook and organize and budget your finances.

Chip: A thin silicon wafer that contains integrated electronic circuits. Chips perform many computer functions including serving as the computer memory.

Click: Pressing the mouse button. This usually refers to the left mouse button. Double click means to press the left mouse button twice in quick succession. Right-click means to press the right mouse button.

Clip Art: Drawings or other images that have been produced to be used in computer programs.

Clipboard: A special area in the computer memory that temporarily stores data which is to be copied to another location.

Clone: A computer that functions exactly like another, better-known product. It is not necessarily an exact copy of that product, but should be able to use the same software and file structures.

Competitive Upgrade: Qualifying to purchase an upgrade

version of a software program because you already own a similar software program from a competing company.

CPU (Central Processing Unit): The main component of a computer system. The *brain* of the computer. Processes all instructions and information.

Cursor (also called the pointer): A symbol, usually a solid rectangle, blinking underline character or arrow that signifies where on the screen the next entry will occur.

Data: Representation of facts, concepts, or instructions.

Database: Collection of information that has been organized in a structured format which can be accessed through a computer system.

Data Bit: (see Bit)

Data Compression: A method of storing data in a format that requires less space than usual.

Decimal System: The most common numbering system based on ten numbers, zero through nine.

Default Settings: The settings that the computer uses at the startup of a program or operating system.

Defragment: The process of taking pieces of files that are scattered or fragmented on the hard disk and unifying them.

Desktop Publishing: The use of computer hardware and software for page layout, typesetting and design.

Diagnostic Software: Software that can help you to determine what is wrong with your computer and correct it.

Disk Fragmentation: (see Fragmentation)

Docking Station: An add-on for a portable computer that allows it to connect to accessories such as monitors and keyboards when it is used as a desktop computer.

Domain Name: When referring to the Internet, the domain name is generally the word or number immediately following the @ sign in an E-mail address.

DOS (Disk Operating System): One of the first operating systems for personal computers.

Dot-matrix Printer: A type of printer that uses the impact of pins striking against an inked ribbon to produce the appropriate characters or shapes.

Download: To move or copy a document, program or other data from the Internet or other computer to your computer. The opposite of upload.

Dpi (Dots per Inch): Way of measuring the density of output of printers and scanners. The higher the dpi, the better the resolution.

DRAM (Dynamic Random Access Memory): The type of RAM used in most personal computers.

DSVD (Digital Simultaneous Voice and Data) Modem: A modem that allows for voice and data to be transferred simultaneously.

Driver: Software that the computer needs to understand how to operate a monitor, printer or other attached device.

Dual-scan: A system of doubling the line that can be changed to speed up the display of an LCD screen

Duplex: Refers to the transmission of data. Full-duplex allows for transmission of data in both directions at the same time. Half-duplex allows for transmission in one direction at one time.

DVD (Digital Video Disc): High density disk that can hold from 4.7 gigabytes to 17 gigabytes of information.

Electromagnetic Radiation: A stream of particles or electromagnetic waves emitted from certain electrical equipment. The long-term effect of these emissions on humans is a matter of speculation at this time.

E-Mail (Electronic Mail): Messages sent to another party through a computer network, such as the Internet.

ENIAC (Electronic Numerical Integrator and Computer): Considered by many to be the first useful computer. Completed in 1946 by John Eckert and John Mauchly.

Enter Key: A key on the computer keyboard that is marked with the word *Enter* or a large arrow. (There is often more than one enter key on the keyboard.) Pressing the enter key will move you down a line in a word processing program. In many programs it completes your selection or your entering of data and sends that data to the computer.

Escape Key: The key marked *esc*. Usually positioned at the upper left of the keyboard. This key often allows you to return to the previous screen.

Ergonomics: The science which studies the safety and comfort of machines and furniture for humans.

Expansion Slots: The slots inside the computer which accept computer boards.

FAQ (Frequently Asked Questions): Compilation of the most commonly asked questions about a certain subject or product.

Fax-back: A service which allows you to order the information of your choice and have that information faxed to you.

Fax-modem: A modem which is designed to send and receive faxes through a computer, as well as act as a regular modem.

Field: A space allocated for a certain type of information.

File: A collection of data.

File Conversion: Changing the formatting of a data file.

File Transfer Protocol: A set of software utilities used to transfer files from one computer to another.

Flame: To send an E-mail or post a message which is assaulting, offensive and/or very aggressive in nature.

Flash BIOS: The BIOS is recorded on a flash memory chip, which can be easily updated if necessary. (see BIOS)

Flat Database: A simple database which is contained in a single table.

Floppy Disk: A thin case enclosing a magnetic disk that stores computer data.

Folder: An object that can hold multiple documents. Used to organize information. Folders can also be called directories.

Font: A collection of letters and numbers in a particular type-face.

Footer: One or more lines of text that appear at the bottom of every page of a document.

Format: (1) The specific arrangement of data (2) To prepare a storage medium, usually a disk, for reading and writing. i.e. to format a floppy disk (3) To specify the properties of an object, i.e. to format the text in a word processing program.

Form Feed: A form feed button or command advances the paper to the beginning of the next page.

Forum: An on-line discussion group where people exchange ideas about a common interest. Also called a newsgroup.

486: An old microprocessor for personal computers. Has been outdated by the introduction of the Pentium chip.

Fragmentation: The condition of a disk in which files are divided into scattered pieces. Fragmentation occurs naturally as you create, modify, and delete files.

Freeware: Copyrighted software given away for free by the author. You can use such software, but cannot sell it in any way.

Frustration: Feelings of discouragement or bewilderment that can be eliminated in the computer world with an understanding of what computers are and how they work.

Function: A type of procedure or routine that is used in programming computers as well as in certain computer programs, such as spreadsheets.

Genealogy Program: A program that helps you to trace your family tree and keep track of all historical familial information.

Gigabyte (GB): A unit of computer storage roughly equaling one billion bytes.

Hacker: Someone, usually knowledgeable about computers, who accesses electronic information without permission.

Hard Disk: The storage disk inside of the computer that holds the operating system and programs.

Hard Drive: The hardware mechanism that contains the hard disk.

Hardware: The physical components of a computer system. Refers to objects like disk drives, monitors, keyboards, and printers.

Header: One or more lines of text that appear at the top of every page of a document.

High-capacity Drive: A floppy disk drive that can hold more information than the average floppy. They are slightly larger than conventional floppy disks, and about twice as thick. They are used for backing up hard disks and for transporting large files.

Hologram: A realistic three-dimensional image that is produced by laser beams.

Home Page: The main page of a Web site.

Hot Link: A link between two application or web pages that allows for easy access between the two. (see Hypertext Link)

HTML (Hypertext Markup Language): The language that is used to create graphic documents for publication on the Web. Documents that are produced with HTML are like text documents that have tags embedded in them. The tags contain coding for attaching graphics, formatting and hypertext links.

HTTP (Hypertext Transfer Protocol): The protocol used by the World Wide Web that defines how messages are formatted and transmitted.

Hypertext Link: A word that you click on when on the Web to take you to another Web page or site. These hot links are usually underlined or in a different color.

IBM-compatible: A computer that provides the same functionality as an IBM PC, but is made by another company. It is capable of running any software that an IBM PC can run.

Icon: A small picture that represents a program, file or command in your computer system. It is activated by moving the cursor onto the icon and pressing a button or key.

Incremental Backup: A backup procedure that backs up only those files that have been changed or modified since the previous backup.

Indent: To set in from the margin. Usually used in the first line of a paragraph.

Industry Standard: When most companies start producing products of a certain type or design, that type or design of the product is said to be the industry standard.

Infrared Port (IrDA, Infrared Data Association): A port that allows the transfer of data from one device to another without any cables via infrared light waves. Both devices must have infrared ports.

Ink Jet Printer: A printer which produces text and images by spraying ink onto the paper. It produces a print out which is close to laser quality at less cost.

Input: (n) Information or data that goes into the computer. This includes information that is typed on the keyboard, as well as information that is gathered from other devices, such as mice or scanners. (v) The act of entering data into a computer.

Installation Disk: A floppy disk or CD-ROM disk which contains the information needed to install a program to the hard disk.

Integrated: Refers to two or more components merged together to work as a single system or as several components that work together seamlessly.

Integrated Pointing Device: A device found in the middle of the keyboard. Used to control the movement of the cursor on the screen. Used instead of a mouse.

Interface: Something that connects two separate entities. It can be either hardware or software. Generally used to refer to the user interface or the part of a software program that connects the computer with a human operator (user).

Interlaced: A type of monitor that produces a certain amount of flickering compared to non-interlaced which reduces that flicker.

Internet: A global web of computers that allows individuals to communicate with each other.

ISDN (Integrated Services Digital Network): A type of online connection that speeds up data transmission by sending data in digital form. Requires a special telephone line.

ISP (Internet Service Provider): A company that lets you dial into their computers in order to connect to the Internet for a fee.

Jaz Drive: A high-capacity disk drive by Iomega Corporation. Holds about 1 GB of data on one removable disk.

Joystick: A lever device similar to a mouse. Basically used to play games on the computer.

Kbps: Kilobits per second (thousands of bits per second). A unit of measurement for modems that indicates the speed at which data is transferred. One kilobit is equal to 1,000 bits.

Keyboard: An input device used to type programs, instructions and data into the computer. Similar to the keys on a typewriter.

Keyboard Shortcut: A keystroke or combination of keystrokes that is used as a substitute for a longer series of keystrokes or mouse clicks.

Laptop Computer: A small, portable computer that can sit on your lap. Laptop computers are often also referred to as notebook computers.

Laser Printer: Printers that produce high quality printouts. They operate like a copy machine, using lasers and toner to produce an image.

LCD (Liquid Crystal Display): The display screens used for most portable computers.

Leading: (pronounced like *ledding*) In word processing and desktop publishing, vertical spacing of lines of text in a paragraph.

Lite Version: A version of the software that does not have all the components that are found in the full version.

Local Bus: A data bus that connects directly, or almost directly, to the microprocessor.

Log On: Before using the Internet or other on-line service you are required to log on. This usually entails entering your user name and password.

Macintosh Computer: A type of computer made by Apple Computer. Macintosh computers are not interchangeable with IBM-compatible computers. They have different microprocessors and file formats. There are many different Macintosh models, with varying degrees of speed and power.

Mail Merge: A system which allows the user to easily generate form letters by automatically inserting each different name and address into the same letter or document.

Marquee: In many programs you can select items by drawing a marquee or box around them. This is usually done by dragging the mouse over the items to be selected.

Megabyte (MB): A unit of computer storage roughly equaling one million bytes.

Megahertz (MHz): Unit of measure used to determine the speed of microprocessors. One MHz represents one million cycles per second. This determines how many instructions per second the microprocessor can execute. For example, a chip that runs at 166MHz executes 166 million cycles per second.

MIDI (Musical Instrument Digital Interface): The protocol for transforming music into data and vise versa. This allows electronic instruments to be attached to and communicate with a computer.

MMX: A set of multimedia instructions built into the microprocessor enabling it to handle many multimedia functions that are normally handled by separate sound and/or video cards.

Modem (Modulator/DEModulator): A device that allows computers to communicate over telephone lines. Modems change the computer's digital signal to an analog signal that can be sent over the telephone lines. Both computers must be equipped with modems in order to communicate.

Monitor: A television-like screen that shows you what your computer is doing.

Mosaic: The first browser for the World Wide Web that was available for many different operating systems. Mosaic started the popularity of the Web.

Motherboard: The main circuit board of the computer.

Mouse: An input device that lets you control the computer by controlling the location and action of the cursor on the computer screen.

MPEG (Motion Pictures Expert Group): One of the standards for compressing full-motion digital video. Requires hardware for decompression.

Netiquette: Rules for maintaining etiquette while using the Internet.

Newsgroup: An on-line discussion group generally geared to a specific topic or group of people.

NFR(Near-Field Recording): A type of mass storage that uses technology similar to a hard disk but which also employs a magneto-optical technology to greatly increase storage capacity.

Notebook Computer: A lightweight portable computer.

OCR (Optical Character Recognition): The process of reading text from paper and translating it into a format that the computer can understand and manipulate.

Off-line: Not connected and therefore unable to communicate.

On-line: Connected and able to communicate.

On-line Banking: Performing normal banking transactions, such as making deposits and paying bills electronically.

On-line Service: A dial-up service, such as CompuServe or America Online, which provides access to the Internet and other electronic services on a subscription basis.

Operating System: A computer program which acts as the link between the computer and the user.

Orientation: In printing, the direction of the paper. Portrait means that the paper is higher than it is wide. Landscape means that the paper is wider than it is high.

OS2: An operating system developed by IBM. Although it is a very good operating system, it never gained enough popularity to become a major operating system.

Output: Anything that comes out of a computer including screen images, printed pages and sounds.

Parallel Port: An interface for connecting external devices, such as printers and scanners.

Parity: The quality of being either odd or even.

Passive-matrix: Flat-screen liquid crystal display (LCD) which consists of energized, rod-shaped crystals that move and bend light. Each pixel either lets light through or blocks it. The direction of the crystals creates the picture. The picture produced is not as clear as an active-matrix display.

Patch: A correction or fix created by a software developer to correct an error in the original program.

PCI (Peripheral Component Interconnect): A local bus standard developed by Intel Corporation.

PCMCIA (Personal Computer Memory Card International Association): A standard that was adapted to enable credit card size devices to be used with computers, especially portable computers. PCMCIA cards are used for modems, hard disks and additional memory.

PDA (Personal Digital Assistant): A handheld device that acts as a mini-computer. It usually combines phone and fax capabilities with a personal organizer and other computer applications.

Pentium: The fifth generation of computer microprocessor chip from Intel Corporation. Previous processors were given numbers, such as 286, 386, 486. Because Intel discovered that it couldn't trademark its CPU numbers, it shifted to a naming scheme, starting with the Pentium processor.

Pentium II: The sixth generation of microprocessor chips from Intel Corporation. Each generation of chips is faster and more powerful.

Peripheral: External device that connects to a computer, such as printer, mouse, scanner and keyboard.

PIM (Personal Information Manager): A type of software that is used to organize information, especially, addresses, to-do lists and appointments.

Pixel (Picture element): A cluster of colored dots that combine to form images on the computer screen.

Plotters: An output device like a printer, which draws lines with pens. Often used in architectural or engineering applications.

Presentation Software: Software that is used to create a series of documents, slides, transparencies or video images and sounds used to exhibit a product or image.

Print Driver: A piece of software that acts as the interface between the computer and the printer. (see Driver)

Printer Self-test: A routine that a printer goes through to show that it is working properly. It usually involves printing a sample sheet without the need to be attached to the computer.

Protocol: A set of standards that allows two products to work together by standardizing communications between the two products.

Public Domain Software: Software that is not copyrighted. It is free and can be used without any restrictions.

RAM (Random Access Memory): The temporary memory of the computer where programs and information are kept. The contents of this memory are lost when the computer is turned off.

Record: In a database, one set of information.

Relational Database: A somewhat complex database which uses several tables that relate to each other in some way.

Reset Button: A button, usually located on the front of the computer, which resets or restarts the computer software without turning the computer completely off.

Resolution: The term used to describe sharpness and clarity of an image. The higher the resolution, the better the image.

ROM (Read Only Memory): Computer memory or disk on which data has been prerecorded. Once data has been written onto a ROM chip or disk, it can only be read and cannot be changed or re-written.

RSI (Repetitive Stress Injuries): An injury that occurs because of a motion that is repeated over and over, causing stress on certain parts of the body.

Scan Disk: A software program, often part of an operating system, which searches the hard disk for errors and corrects them.

Scanner: A device that takes a picture of a printed page or image and puts it into the computer memory.

Screen Saver: A software program that runs some sort of animation on the computer screen when it is turned on, but not in use.

SCSI (Small Computer System Interface): A high-speed interface that is used for hard drives, scanners and other devices.

Search and Replace: Part of a software program which allows you to search for certain words, phrases or characters and replace them with other words, phrases or characters.

Self-test: (see Printer Self-test)

Serial Port: A port or interface used for serial communication. It can only transfer one bit at a time. Used for modems, mice and occasionally, printers.

Server: A computer or device that manages network resources. A file server is a computer and storage device that is used for storing files. A print server is a computer that manages one or more printers.

Service Release: A compilation of software patches that are released by the software manufacturer as a group.

Shareware: Software that is sold by a company or individual for a nominal fee. It can be copied freely for a trial basis. If you decide to use the shareware program you are expected to pay for it.

Skew: To turn or place an object at an angle. Often used in drawing programs to manipulate pictures or drawings.

Software: The program or instructions that tell the computer what to do.

Software Licenses: Nearly all software applications are licensed rather than sold. There are many different types of software licenses. Most personal computer software licenses allow you to run the program on one machine and to make copies of the software only for backup purposes. Some licenses also allow you to run the program on different computers as long as you don't use the copies simultaneously, or with other restrictions.

Software Piracy: Unauthorized copying of software.

Sound Card: An internal card in the computer, which when attached to the PC speaker or external speakers, allows the computer to produce audio sounds.

Spam: To send unwanted E-mail or messages to several recipients. The electronic equivalent of junk mail.

SRAM (Static Random Access Memory): A type of memory that is faster and more reliable than the more common DRAM.

Start Bit: In asynchronous communications, a bit that indicates that a byte has just been transmitted. Each byte of data is preceded by a start bit and followed by a stop bit.

Startup Disk: A floppy disk that contains the information that is necessary to start the computer when the hard drive is not functioning properly.

Stop Bits: (see Start Bit)

Stylus: A pencil-shaped instrument that is used as an input device.

Sub-notebook Computer: A portable computer that is smaller than a notebook computer.

Subwoofer: A speaker which can reproduce sound at the lowest end of the sound spectrum.

Suite: A group of programs that are sold together as one unit for a price less than the cost of the individual components.

Surge Protector: A device that protects electronic equipment from power surges or spikes.

SVGA (Super Video Graphics Array): A set of graphics standards that have better resolution than VGA. Included resolutions range from 800 by 600 pixels to 1600 by 1200 pixels.

Tab: A mechanism for setting automatic stops or margins in order to line up text or items in columns.

Table: A collection of related data in a database.

Tape Drive: An internal or external computer drive which uses tape as the medium for reading and writing data. Since a tape must be accessed sequentially, tape drives are much slower than most other data-access methods.

Technical Support: Support that is given to the computer hardware or software user from the manufacturer of the equipment or developer of the software. This includes help in installing and using the products.

Technophobia: A fear of technology.

Template: A pattern that is used to create other like items. Often used to create documents that are similar, but have small differences.

Thermal Dye Transfer Printer: A printer that transforms the ink into a gas which hardens on the page to produce high quality color images that look like photos. Also called dye sublimation printer.

Thermal Wax Printer: A printer that uses colored wax, heated and melted onto the paper to produce colors.

Toolbar: A strip of icons in a software program that usually are located at the top of the screen.

Toner: The type of ink used in laser printers and copy machines. It is a dry powder.

Touchpad: An input device that consists of a small touch-sensitive pad. The user moves his or her finger across the pad to move the cursor on the screen.

Track Ball: An input device used in place of a mouse which has a ball that is moved with the fingers to direct the movement of the cursor on the computer screen.

Tracking: In word processing or desktop publishing, to adjust the space between the characters of type.

Troubleshoot: To systematically investigate a problem and find a solution.

Typeface: A collection of letters, numbers and symbols that have the same distinctive appearance.

Undo Button: The icon or button in a software application that allows you to reverse, or undo your last action.

Uninstaller: A software program which removes or uninstalls other programs.

UNIX: An operating system that runs many of the large computer systems.

Upgrade: To improve your computer system by installing new components. Also to install a new version of the software that you are already using to gain new features and improvements.

Upload: To move or copy a document, program or other data from your computer to the Internet or another computer. The opposite of download.

UPS (Uninterrupted Power Supply): A power supply that includes a battery to maintain power in case of a power outage or gap.

URL (Uniform Resource Locator): A system for addressing Internet sites.

USB (Universal Serial Bus): A hardware bus standard that allows users to plug a peripheral into a USB port and have it automatically configured and ready to use.

Usenet: A worldwide bulletin board system that can be accessed through the Internet or through many on-line services. It contains thousands of newsgroups that cover many varied topics.

Utility Programs: A program that helps you perform necessary maintenance or correct problems with your computer system. Disk backup and anti-virus programs are utility programs.

Version: A new version of a software or hardware product is designed to replace an older version of the same product adding new and/or updated features.

VGA (Video Graphics Array): The minimum standard for monitor resolution: 640 by 480 pixels.

Virtual Reality: An artificial environment created by computer hardware and software which appears and feels like a real environment.

Virus: An unwanted file or set of instructions that replicates and attaches itself to files in your computer system, usually causing harm to your computer.

Voice Modem: A modem which is capable of processing voice as well as computer data. In data mode, the modem acts like a regular modem. In voice mode, the modem acts like a regular telephone.

Voice Recognition: Software which allows the computer to recognizes the spoken word in much the same way that a secretary would take dictation. With voice recognition, the computer can also perform certain functions in response to the spoken word.

VRAM (Video Random-Access Memory): Memory used by video adapters. It can be accessed by two different devices simultaneously enabling faster screen redraws and faster access of graphic material than regular RAM. This type of memory helps the computer RAM process video images.

Wave Table: Uses recordings of actual instruments to produce sound that is more accurate and of better quality than an ordinary soundboard.

Web Browser: A program that provides an interface that allows you to connect to the World Wide Web.

Web Page: One area of the World Wide Web. Comparable to a page in a book.

Wizard: An assistant or helper created by a software program to help the user perform tasks.

Word Processor: A piece of software used to create documents which are text oriented.

World Wide Web: A graphical interface for the Internet

Zip Disks: A removable disk that holds more information than a floppy. A 100MB zip disk holds about 70 times the amount of information on a high-density 3$\frac{1}{2}$" floppy disk.

Zip Drive: A device for storing information on a type of floppy disk which is much higher density than a floppy.

Index

D

data compression, 169, 170
database, 158
database, flat, 159
database, relational, 159
decimal numbering system, 20
default, 72
defragmentation, 107
desktop publishing, 179
diagnostic software, 60
Digital Simultaneous Voice and
    Data. See DSVD
Digital VideoDiscs. See DVD
discernment, 207
docking station, 81
domain name, 200, 201
DOS, 24, 25, 106, 107, 170, 174
dot matrix printers, 119
dot pitch, 33
download, 188
DRAM, 34
drawing programs, 178
DSVD, 44
dust, 95
DVD, 36, 214
Dynamic RAM. See DRAM

E

Eckert, John, 18
Edison, Thomas Alva, 27
edit menu, 74
Einstein, Albert, 9
electromagnetic radiation, 33
Electronic mail. See E-mail
E-mail, 198, 199, 202
Emerson, Ralph Waldo, 179
emoticoms, 203
encyclopedia, 166
Engelbart, Douglas, 41
ENIAC, 18, 19
ergonomic, 40, 56, 62
escape, 64
exit, 106
expansion slots, 45

eyestrain, 57

F

FAQ, 114
fax, 190
fax-back, 113
fax-modem, 43
field, 159
file compression, 189
file conversion, 179
file names, 76
file transfer protocol, 188
files, 73
flame, 202
Flash BIOS, 46
floppy disk, 38, 98
flying programs, 175
font, 154
Forbes, Malcolm, 91
Ford, Henry, 81
form feed, 125
formatting, 155
formatting a disk, 38
forums, 192
fragmentation. See defragmentation
Frankston, Bob, 156
freeware, 137
frequently asked questions. See
    FAQ
Franklin, Benjamin, 23
frustration, 69
functions, 157

G

games, 173
games, board, 182
genealogy programs, 176
glare, 55, 57
Goethe, Johann, 100
Grove, Andy, 211

H

Halle, Salmon, 50
hard disk, 31, 99, 100, 106, 107,
    108, 168, 169, 170
hard disk maintenance, 106

hard drive, 31, 63, 99, 101, 105, 168
hardware, 21
heat, 94
help screens, 68
high-density drive, 40
history of computers, 17
Holland, Josiah, 166
hologram, 217
home page, 197
hot links, 167
HTML, 195, 197
HTTP, 195
Hugo, Victor, 13
humidity, 94
Hypertext Transfer Protocol, 195

I

Iacocca, Lee, 49
IBM compatible, 25, 29
identification, 216
incremental backup system, 102
infrared ports., 86
ink jet printers, 120
installing, 147
integrated, 151
integrated circuit, 28
integrated pointing device, 84
Intel, 28, 29, 211
interface, 167
interlaced, 32
Internet, 190, 204
Internet Service Provider, 194
investment tracking, 163
ISDN, 43

J

jaz drive, 40
Jefferson, Thomas, 63
Jerome, Jerome, 151
joysticks, 134
Jung, Carl, 117

K

Kbps, 43
keyboard, 40

keyboard shortcut, 75
kilobits per second. See Kbps

L

label printer, 123
language programs, 166
laptop, 82
laser printer, 121
LCD, 85
license agreement, 145
lightning, 92
liquid crystal display. See LCD
lite version, 142
local bus, 35

M

Macintosh. See Apple computers
magnetism, 99, 101
mail merge, 156
mail-order buying, 52
mass storage units, 39
Mauchly, John, 18
megahertz, 29, 30
memory, 30
microphone, 37
Microsoft Network, 193
MIDI, 185
Mishna, 190
Mizner, Wilson, 36
MMX, 29
modem, 43, 187, 188
modem, external, 44
modem, internal, 44
monitor, 32, 33
Monopoly, 182
Montaigne, 55
Mosaic, 196
motherboard, 28
Motion Pictures Expert Group. See MPEG
Motorola, 29
mouse, 41, 97
movie programs, 180
MPEG, 35
MPR II standards, 33

287

Murphy's Law, 77
music programs, 185

N

near-field recording. See NFR
netiquette, 201
newsgroups, 205
NFR, 32
non-interlaced, 32
notebook, 82

O

OCR, 131
off-line, 187
on-line, 111, 187
on-line service, 191
on-line support, 113
operating system, 21, 24
optical character recognition. See
        OCR
orientation, 155
OS2, 26

P

painting programs, 178
parallel port, 44
Pascal, Blaise, 17
passive-matrix, 86
patch, 143
PCMCIA, 84
Pentium, 28, 29, 30
Pentium Pro, 28, 30
peripheral, 44, 59, 70, 81, 98, 136
Personal Computer Memory Card
International Association. See
        PCMCIA
personal digital assistants, 88
personal information managers, 160
photo programs, 181
piracy, 146
pixel, 86
plotter, 123
pointing stick. See integrated
        pointing device
points, 154
popularity, 140

port, 44
portable computers, 81
Power PC, 29
presentation software, 160
print driver, 125
printer self-test, 111
printer troubleshooting, 111,125
printers, 118
processor speed, 29
Prodigy, 193
public domain, 137

R

RAM, 30
Random Access Memory. See
RAM
read only memory. See ROM
record, 159
register, 61
reliability ratings, 50
repetitive stress injuries. See RSI
resolution, 122, 129
ROM, 36
RSI, 56
Russell, Bertrand, 14

S

scan disk, 107
scanner, 127
scanner, color, 130
scanner, flatbed, 129
scanner, hand-held, 128
scanner, photo, 132
scanner, sheet feed, 128
screen saver, 105
SCSI, 129
search and replace, 156
search engine, 214
serial port, 44
service release, 144
shareware, 137
Shaw, George Bernard, 41
simplification, 9, 213
Small Computer System Interface.
        See SCSI

smoke, 95
software, 21
software license. See license agree
ment
Soulas, Lenor, 137
Sound Blaster-compatible, 37
sound card, 37
soundboard. See sound card
spam, 202
speakers, 37
spreadsheet, 156
start up disk, 60
static electricity, 94, 101
sub-notebook, 82
subwoofer, 38
suite, 142, 151
super VGA, 32
surge protector, 91

T

table, 159
tape drive, 102
tax programs, 165
technical support, 51, 111
technophobia, 14
template, 156
thermal dye transfer printers, 123
thermal wax color printers, 122
touchpad, 84
track ball, 83
transistor, 27, 28, 86
travel, 177
Twain, Mark, 69

U

undo, 64
Uniform Resource Locator, 198
uninstaller, 170
uninterrupted power supply. See
UPS
UNIX, 24, 25
unpack the computer, 58
upgrade, 142
upload, 188
UPS, 94

URL, 198
USB (Universal Serial Bus), 45
utility programs, 168

V

versions, 141
VGA, 32
video board, 34
video memory, 34
video RAM, 34
virtual reality, 173, 217
virus, 109
VisiCalc, 156
voice modem, 42, 44
voice recognition, 38
VRAM, 34

W

warranties, 51
wave table, 37
web browser, 196
web page, 196
Windows NT, 26
wizard, 68, 155
word processing, 152, 155
World Wide Web, 195

Y

Yates, William Butler, 187

Z

zip drive, 40, 102
zipped file, 189